James McNair's **New Pizza**

James McNair's **New Pizza**

Foolproof Techniques and Fabulous Recipes

By James McNair
Photographs by Joyce Oudkerk Pool

CHRONICLE BOOKS
SAN FRANCISCO

For Carol Gallagher, a great friend and naturalized cousin, who has added much pleasure to my life, and who knows how to turn my meaty recipes into vegetarian delights.

And in memory of my father, James Odis McNair (1914–1999), who always gave his love through the joys and sorrows of my life, and who helped teach me to cook and even learned to like pizza over the years.

Acknowledgments

Library of Congress Cataloging-in-Publication Data:
McNair, James.
    James McNair's new pizza: foolproof techniques and fabulous recipes/ by James McNair; photographs by Joyce Oudkerk Pool.
        p. cm.
    Includes index.
    ISBN 0-8118-2364-4
    1. Pizza   II. Title.

    TX770.P58 M3597 2000
    641.8'24—dc21
                99-086781
                CIP
Printed in Hong Kong.

Prop styling by Carol Hacker/Tableprop
Food styling by Andrea Lucich
Designed by Shawn Hazen

Distributed in Canada by
Raincoast Books
9050 Shaughnessy Street
Vancouver, British Columbia V6P 6E5

10 9 8 7 6 5 4 3 2 1

Chronicle Books
85 Second Street
San Francisco, California 94105

www.chroniclebooks.com

To Bill LeBlond, my editor at Chronicle Books, for giving me the opportunity to write about one of my favorite subjects one more time, and to assistant editor Stephanie Rosenbaum for her good work.

To Sharon Silva, copy editor for most of my projects with Chronicle Books, for her skillful honing of my words.

To Joyce Oudkerk Pool, photographer, and Carol Hacker and Andrea Lucich, stylists, for interpreting my recipes on film.

To Shawn Hazen, graphic designer, for creating such an attractive package for my work.

To my family and friends for their encouragement throughout this project, especially those who shared pizzas and opinions during the testing phase. Special thanks to my mother, Lucille McNair; my sister, Martha McNair; my brother-in-law, John Richardson; and my nephews, Devereux McNair and Ryan Richardson, for their love and support as we shared in mourning the death of my father during the writing of this book. And to Almut and Rolf Busch and John Carr for looking after my San Francisco home while I was in hibernation at Lake Tahoe to complete this book.

To Beauregard Ezekiel Valentine, Miss Vivien "Bunny" Fleigh, Miss Olivia de Puss Puss, Joshua J. Chew, and Michael T. Wigglebutt, my four-legged companions, for hanging out during the baking of hundreds of test pizzas in hopes of sharing the results.

To Andrew Moore, my devoted partner, for his usual brilliance in conceptualizing and refining both the words and pizzas for this book.

The photography staff wishes to thank Julie Sanders of Cyclamen and all our friends and family for their support.

Contents

Pizza: Past, Present, and Future

The popularity of pizza is thriving like never before in its amazingly long history. Today in the United States alone over 4 billion fresh pizzas are ordered each year from the countless pizzerias that dot every community. No longer restricted to chain operations, upscale versions of the humble pie can be found on the menus of our finest restaurants. Another 1.1 billion frozen pizzas are sold annually. Millions more of us prefer the even better taste of pizza freshly made in our own kitchens.

The modern pizza traces its heritage to the various versions of seasoned flat breads that were first created about three millennia ago in the civilizations that flourished around the Mediterranean Sea, including Egypt, Mesopotamia, and Greece. Residents of the region now known as Tuscany have been eating some form of pizza since the Etruscans settled there around 1000 B.C. The mighty Roman civilization adopted the idea from the Etruscans and the Greeks who had occupied the southern part of what is now Italy. The water buffalo arrived along with the invaders that followed the fall of the Roman Empire, and mozzarella cheese made from its milk eventually redefined the pizza.

By A.D. 1000, a mere two millennia after the inception of seasoned flat breads, *picea,* a disk of dough generously dusted with herbs and spices, was common in Naples, the Italian port city that claims pizza as its own invention. The simple pie was often a snack for the women who needed to satisfy hunger pangs while waiting for their bread to bake in the town's communal oven. A *signora* would break off a piece of the dough, flatten it out, and top it with whatever seasonings were on hand, then quickly bake it in the hot oven.

Writers throughout the Middle Ages and the Renaissance mention various types of pizza that appeared on the tables of both the nobility and peasants. The earliest pizzas were baked without today's ubiquitous tomato crown. Although the tomato plant had been introduced to Italian gardens from Peru via Spain by the 1520s, it was grown strictly as an ornamental because its fruits were considered poisonous. The earliest plants produced bright yellow tomatoes that were known as *pomodori,* or "golden apples." Tomatoes were finally added to the Italian kitchen in 1750, altering the course of pizza forever.

Despite the fact that Italian home bakers turned out pizzas for centuries, it was not until the mid-eighteenth century that pizza became a commercial staple of Naples. Pizza bakeries sprang up throughout the city and young men transported the freshly baked pies in hot metal boxes, hawking their wares up and down the streets. In 1830, the first modern pizzeria, Pizzeria Port' Alba, was opened in the city, and its wood-fired oven was lined with lava rock from nearby Mount Vesuvius. This venerable institution remains in business today.

An important event in the popularization of pizza occurred in 1889, when King Umberto I of Savoy, on a wedding tour of his kingdom, arrived in Naples with his young bride, Queen Margherita. Tired of the rich court food, the queen asked to sample some of the popular foods of the people. Raffaele Esposito, considered the premier pizza baker of the time, was summoned to prepare pizzas for the queen. He ran the successful Pizzeria e Basta Cosí, also known by the nickname of its founder, Pietro il Pizzaiolo, or "Peter the Pizza Baker," which opened in 1780 as a pizza stand, and it remains in operation today as the bustling Pizzeria Brandi. Esposito and his wife, Maria Giovanna Brandi, arrived at the royal palace of Capo di Monte on their donkey-drawn cart and prepared three types of pies, all favorites of his customers.

In my first book on pizza, I repeated the long-circulated story that chef Esposito invented a special combination that day: tomato, mozzarella, and basil to capture the red, white, and green of the Italian flag in honor of the queen. Culinary historians now point out that this combination was already popular among Neapolitans prior to the queen's pizza delivery. Of the three types of pizzas that Esposito prepared for his queen, however, she liked this combination the best. From that day on, this simple preparation, still one of the world's best-loved pizzas, has been known as pizza Margherita in her honor.

Today, in an effort to preserve the authentic pizza of Naples, the Association of Verace Pizza Napoletana has been formed. Their certification is awarded exclusively to pizzerias whose pies fulfill rigid standards for ingredients, mixing, shaping, and baking. Crusts may contain only flour, natural yeast or yeast of beer, salt, and water. These simple ingredients must be mixed by hand or with an association-approved machine that prevents the dough from over-heating during mixing or kneading. After rising, the dough must be shaped by hand without the use of a rolling pin or any mechanical means. The pie must be placed directly on the volcanic-stone floor of a bell-shaped wood-burning brick oven that is heated to a temperature of 750 to 800 degrees F. The finished product must be soft, well cooked, and fragrant, with the toppings enclosed in a high, soft edge of crust. Variations on traditional toppings must not be "in contrast with the rules of gastronomy."

In a guidebook to Naples, published by the local chamber of commerce, Mario Stefanile praises the port city's main claim to culinary fame with this dare: "Yet just try and make it anywhere

made beyond the boot, but I firmly believe that the peasant pie has reached at least equal, if not greater, heights in North America. When made by a skilled chef or good home cook who masters the simple art of making crusts and practices restraint with toppings, the North American pizza can be sublime.

Pizza arrived on our shores along with the first wave of Italian immigrants during the late nineteenth century, and Gennaro Lombardi opened the first American pizzeria at 53⅓ Spring Street in New York City in 1905, where he served a variation of the Neapolitan pie. Pizza remained restricted to the Italian neighborhoods of American cities until the end of World War II, when soldiers returning from duty in Italy were intent upon introducing it to their friends and families. Demand soon pushed the pizzeria into new areas where it could cater to the general public, who quickly learned to love the pie. The first chain, Pizza Hut, debuted in Kansas City in 1958, followed in 1960 by Domino's in Detroit.

North Americans have the highest rate of pizza consumption per capita of any place in the world. In fact, pizza sales here account for more than 10 percent of all prepared food sales.

other than Naples. Just try and mix the flour with water that is not from the Serino, or have the dough flattened by anyone other than a *pizzaiolo*, one of the heirs to a tradition that goes back into the recesses of time. Just try to make it without local olive oil or lard, or tomatoes that have not ripened between the Sebeto and the Sele, or crown it with *basilico* that hasn't grown under the sun of Naples; try to place it in the oven without that certain lilting, rhythmic step. As for the oven, it must be as large as a room, ardent as the blood that flows through the veins of a young girl, and burning bundles of the very driest vine branches that barely leave ashes. Without all of this, what kind of pizza could you ever hope to obtain?"

While I admit that the pizzas of Naples are indeed wonderful, and while I certainly don't wish to offend Mr. Stefanile and his fellow defenders of the Neapolitan pie, I don't think that pizza is solely the province of the Neapolitan baker, or of Italy for that matter. Of course, I am the first to acknowledge that many poor imitations are

Within my lifetime, pizza has grown from an obscure item known only in scattered immigrant communities to North America's favorite food. My own discovery of the comforting pleasures of pizza took place in New York City, since the exotic pie had yet to make inroads into my native Louisiana by the time I left home. Before then I'd only eaten pizza a few times: the version rendered by a not-very-good New Orleans pizzeria, and my adolescent sister's interpretations of a mix from the grocer's shelves. My very first dinner in the Big Apple was at Al Buon Gusto, a Columbus Avenue pizzeria just around the corner from my West Seventy-second Street apartment. During my subsequent years in New York, I repeated that short trip countless times.

One day, when my family was visiting from Louisiana, my daddy volunteered to go around the corner for take-out pizza. He was gone for what seemed like a very long time just to pick up a few slices, which were always available ready to go from the pizzeria. When I finally opened the door upon his return, there he stood, grinning and blushing at his obvious mistake, holding a stack of five enormous pizza boxes. Having little knowledge about the culture of the pizzeria and always wanting to make sure that there was plenty of food on our table, he'd ordered one large pie for each person. Needless to say, we munched leftover pizza until we couldn't look at another piece. My father died at the age of eighty-five while I was writing this book, and during the immense sadness that surrounded this event in my family, we all enjoyed a much-needed laugh as we remembered that long-ago New York pizza surplus.

I'll also never forget a lucky chance encounter with pizza on my first trip to Italy. I was traveling with my friend Lenny Meyer and Venice was our initial stop. A sudden downpour forced us to duck under the canopy of a tiny pizzeria for protection. Since we were trapped there, we thought we might as well order the house specialty. It was my first pizza in the country of its origin, and I thought that I had arrived in heaven when I bit into the thin, crisp crust and the light shower of fresh simple ingredients. The crusts became a bit thicker and the pizzas only got better as I traveled south.

In the years since those early experiences with pizza, I've made thousands of pizzas in every size, shape, and flavor. In addition to my homebaked pies, I've sampled pizza in every guise, from those baked in tiny, hole-in-the-wall pizzerias to offbeat versions in trendy, upscale restaurants. This book is my definitive sharing of what I've learned from my own trials, errors, and accomplishments, along with both scholarly and practical research on the subject.

In starting my third book on pizza, I questioned just what it is about this simple dish that has raised it from relative obscurity to wild popularity within my lifetime. Perhaps the best answer is that nothing smells or tastes better than hot, yeasty bread served directly from the oven. When that fabulous crust of bread is topped with melted cheese and a few flavor-packed ingredients, it becomes the ultimate comfort food. And I can't think of a more sociable repast. Just place a hot pizza in the center of a table and watch it break down any barrier to conversation and appeal to every taste, just as it has for the last three millennia.

Whether you are an avid devotee of the art of home pizza baking or a novice in the kitchen, this book will arm you with surefire techniques for turning out pies that rival both the staples of Naples and the versions from our trendiest chefs. Use my ideas as a home base for inventing new favorites and refining Old World classics.

How to Use This Book

Before making any of the pizzas, please read pages 9–25 for detailed directions on every step of the process—from making the dough through slicing the finished pie. I begin the directions for each recipe with a statement urging you to review the fundamentals if necessary. Once you've made a few pizzas, you will not need to look back at those directions each time.

In most of the pizza recipes, I have not specified the shape or size of the crust or the number of pizzas to make. Using the directions on page 21, take your choice of a single large pizza for sharing, individual ones, or appetizer-sized *pizzette*. Each recipe makes enough crust and toppings for eight servings. Keep in mind that most people will eat two servings of pizza as a main course, but only a single serving as an appetizer.

I prefer crusts that are neither cracker thin nor too thick. I usually make them about $1/4$ inch thick with a rim of about $1/2$ inch, or about the thickness of the classic Neapolitan pizza. The amount of topping suggested in each recipe will cover that size adequately. If making multiple pizzas with a batch of dough, divide the toppings evenly among them. If you make thinner crusts, you may end up with larger pizzas that need a bit more topping. If you prefer thick crusts, you may end up with a little too much topping. The ratio is very subjective, but whether following a recipe or creating your own pizzas, be certain not to overload the crust with too many conflicting elements or pile it up with too much of a good thing.

Unless you have a large oven or multiple ovens, plan on baking only one large pizza at a time. Most baking stones can accommodate two individual pizzas simultaneously. You can also use several screens that are only slightly larger than the pizzas and place as many as will fit comfortably on the top rack of the oven without crowding. Most ovens will hold a single large screen or ventilated pan or a pair of individual-sized pizza screens or pans.

Making Perfect Pizza at Home

Before starting to make a pizza, please read this section through several times in order to understand the steps necessary for creating all sizes and types. Once you fully grasp the various elements—mixing, kneading, shaping, and baking—of pizza making, the process will be quite easy. With just a little practice, you will be quickly turning out the most scrumptious pizzas you've ever tasted and creating your own countless variations.

9

Ingredients

For the best pizzas, the rule is simple: use only the freshest and finest ingredients available.

Flours

When wheat flour is mixed with water, two different types of protein in the flour search out and connect with their own kind. As the mixture is stirred or kneaded, these proteins combine to form sheets of gluten. The sheets encapsulate the gases that are created by the action of living yeast and trap the air that results from kneading the mixture. The protein content of flour determines how much gluten will be formed, and the amount of gluten determines how much the dough will rise, as well as defines the final texture of the pizza, which can range from soft to chewy.

In Italian pizzerias, a silken flour, finely milled from soft winter wheat, is prized for its low gluten content. It produces the soft, tender crust characteristic of Neapolitan pizzas. The closest North American counterparts are cake flour and bleached Southern all-purpose flour, both finely milled from soft red winter wheat. To build up the gluten in their dough and to ensure the desired chewy texture, Italian bakers add North American all-purpose flour to their soft flour. They use either American all-purpose flour, a blend of soft and hard red winter wheat, or the Canadian all-purpose flour known as Manitoba, a blend of soft and hard wheat with a high protein content. If you wish to emulate the crust of Naples, look for imported Italian flour at gourmet grocers such as Dean & DeLuca, or purchase readily available plain cake flour, finely milled from soft red winter wheat. Avoid self-rising cake flour that contains baking powder and salt. Combine the soft flour with unbleached all-purpose flour in the ratio suggested in the recipe for Neapolitan-Style Pizza Dough on page 16. If you prefer a softer crust, adjust the mixture in favor of the imported or cake flour. For a chewier crust, increase the percentage of all-purpose flour.

At the opposite end of the pizza crust spectrum are the firmer-textured crusts that can be stretched quite thin and baked extra-crisp. To make these, choose bread flour made from hard northern spring wheat. This is the flour used by most American pizzerias. The high protein content of bread flour raises yeast dough to its maximum volume. Semolina flour, the same type used in quality dried pasta, is milled from hard durum wheat, and the dough made from it generally requires the addition of a little more water than is necessary with other flours. Look for a finely milled version. Dough made of semolina or bread flour takes longer to knead and rise than dough made with all-purpose flour, but the resulting crisp crusts may make the extra effort and time worthwhile if you prefer thin, crackerlike crusts.

Most of the time I reach for readily available American all-purpose flour. It makes excellent pizza crusts with a texture somewhere between the soft and chewy Neapolitan style and the crisp style yielded by bread flour. Dough made with all-purpose flour requires less moisture, kneading, and rising time than dough made with bread or semolina flour. If you favor a chewy character, use the unbleached type. For a softer, moister crust, choose bleached flour.

The exact amount of flour you'll end up kneading into the dough depends on the type of flour used and the amount of moisture in the air. When humidity is high, the dough will be sticky and you will need to add more flour. If the dough is too dry, you must add extra water; be sure to add it only a small bit at a time to prevent the dough from becoming too wet.

Salt

For a full and balanced flavor, salt is an essential ingredient in pizza dough. I now use about twice the amount that I called for in my first pizza book, which was written during the time of our national, and sometimes irrational, fear of salt. If using coarse kosher or sea salts with large crystals, first grind them in a salt mill or electric spice grinder so they will melt properly in the dough.

Yeast

In order to rise, pizza dough, like other breads, requires the carbon dioxide produced by yeast, microscopic living organisms that can be stored in a dormant state until moisture is added. My pizza dough recipes are written for using active dry yeast in either its regular form or the quick-rising version, both readily available from supermarkets in premeasured 1/4-ounce packets or in bulk in glass jars. The quick-rising version cuts the rising time of dough by about 20 percent, but some commercial bakers complain that the dough develops less flavor.

Because I use a lot of dry yeast, I prefer to purchase it in bulk in glass jars. Once opened, store the remaining yeast in the tightly sealed glass jar in a cool, dry place, or in the refrigerator or freezer for up to six months. Always use a clean, dry measuring spoon when retrieving yeast, to avoid getting any moisture into the remaining yeast that could activate it. Many baking experts advocate returning refrigerated or frozen yeast to room temperature before using, but I've found that the temperature of the yeast makes no difference in the proofing or rising time.

Although my recipes call for dry yeast, compressed fresh moist yeast cakes can be used in its place by substituting a .06-ounce cake for one packet of dry yeast. Fresh yeast is highly perishable and should be kept refrigerated for up to two weeks.

Another type of yeast, instant yeast, has been available to commercial bakers for several decades, but it is a relatively new product for home bakers. As it is a more highly active strain of yeast than that used in regular dry yeast, a bit less may be required for good rising. Instant yeast does not have to be dissolved in water before it is added to the other dough ingredients. If you choose instant yeast, available from bread-supply catalogs and some specialty markets, use the amount recommended by the manufacturer to replace regular yeast and combine it with the flour and salt, then add the water and oil (if using). Store instant yeast as directed on the package.

No matter which type you choose, always check the expiration dates on yeast packages, and unless you are absolutely certain the yeast is fresh, it should be proofed to determine that it is still active. To proof yeast, dissolve it in warm water with a bit of sugar to feed it as directed in the pizza dough recipe introductions.

Water

If your tap water has a high chlorine and/or fluoride content, use a water purifier or purchase spring water, as the additives not only affect the flavor of pizza dough but also may inhibit proper development of the yeast. The water temperature must be warm to the touch, never too hot or cold. An instant-read thermometer inserted into the water should register between 110 and 115 degrees F.

Oils

Although not traditional with bakers of Neapolitan or New York–style pizzas, the addition of olive oil, or sometimes another oil, to pizza dough creates a flavorful crust with a tender interior. Whether oil is mixed into the dough or not, it should be brushed on the crust before baking to keep it from drying out in the oven and to ensure a golden brown color and delicious flavor. I also like to swab the edges of the crust with oil as soon as the pizza comes out of the oven to add a little moisture, shine, and flavor.

The nature of olive oil varies according to the method by which it was produced. Extra-virgin olive oil is the highest quality and therefore the most expensive. To produce it, the finest olives are pressed by hand. As I prefer its rich green color and fresh olive flavor, it is the oil that I heartily recommend for pizzas. It is not necessary, however, to purchase costly boutique olive oil in beautiful bottles for making pizza. Save those precious oils for salads or for dipping bread where their complex flavors will best be appreciated, and instead use a readily available national brand of oil that is green and tastes like the fruit. If you prefer a lighter-tasting olive oil, look for one with a golden color in bottles labeled "olive oil." Such oils are produced from the second or third pressing of the olives.

I use bland or lightly flavored vegetable oil for greasing screens and pans and in the dough when olive oil would overwhelm or be incompatible with the toppings. For variety in nontraditional pizzas, choose intensely flavored walnut oil, Asian toasted sesame oil, roasted peanut oil, chile oil, or a favorite flavored olive oil. Look for these oils in well-stocked supermarkets, gourmet specialty shops, and Asian markets. Just be sure that the selected oil smells fresh and is compatible, not competitive, with the toppings.

Cheeses

Although you can make good pizzas without it, cheese in some form is an essential ingredient to what most of us envision as a perfect pizza. It may be as light as a sprinkling of imported Parmesan after the pie comes out of the oven, or as rich as a blend of smooth-melting cheeses merging with the crust.

Mozzarella is the most common cheese used in pizza making. It is available in two forms: fresh packed in water and semisoft sealed in plastic. In Italy, fresh mozzarella, especially the variety made by hand in part from water buffalo's milk, is the choice of many pizza bakers and is essential if you wish to capture authentic Neapolitan flavor. Imported versions are available, alongside tubs of domestic counterparts made from cow's milk, in cheese shops and upscale markets in the United States. Some versions of fresh mozzarella may not melt quite as smoothly as the factory-made semisoft mozzarella most Americans are accustomed to using. High-fat versions of fresh mozzarella melt quickly and can burn before the pizza is done. When using such cheese, unless it is drizzled with olive oil or topped by another ingredient, such as tomatoes, it may be best to wait until the pizza is approximately half-baked before adding the cheese. If you locate these fresh cheeses but can't use them the same day, store them for up to a couple of days immersed in a solution of water mixed with a little fat-free milk; change the solution daily.

Unfortunately, most semisoft mozzarella, especially the readily available low-moisture type made from part nonfat milk and developed by cheese processors for the commercial pizza industry, melts into a rubbery mass that leaves long strings trailing from the mouth to the piece of pizza. While this is some people's idea of a good pizza, I use whole-milk mozzarella, which is made by a few high-quality manufacturers throughout the United States. It melts smoothly with none of those annoying rubbery strings. I also prefer its smooth texture to fresh mozzarella on most pizzas, except when I'm replicating a Neapolitan classic. Keep in mind, however, that most American mass-produced mozzarella has very little flavor in comparison with the original Italian version.

If you don't have access to high-quality mozzarella, here are a few tips to prevent mass-produced supermarket versions from becoming rubbery. Shred or chop the cheese instead of slicing it; it will melt more smoothly. Marcella Hazan, doyenne of Italian cooking, advocates soaking the shredded mozzarella in olive oil for about an hour before cooking to approximate the creaminess of its fresh counterpart. Blending mozzarella with other good-melting cheeses also results in a creamier melt. I often mix mozzarella with Italian Fontina or provolone, Dutch Gouda, French Gruyère, Vermont Cheddar, California Monterey Jack, or any other cheese that melts nicely. Often I forget the mozzarella entirely and use other cheeses in combination or alone. Be adventuresome and try your favorites. Chances are they'll work.

I often finish off a fresh-from-the-oven pizza with Parmesan cheese. If you don't go with top-of-the-line Parmigiano-Reggiano, which is costly but definitely worth it, choose the best similar grating cheese that you can find. Italy protects her superior products with restricted labeling; similar Italian cheeses must be marked *grana*. Some cheeses produced outside of Italy are labeled Parmesan but bear little resemblance to the classic. Other dry cheeses, such as Asiago, dry Jack, or a few domestic "Parmesans," are decent substitutes, but don't even think of using that stuff out of a green box on one of my pizzas!

Tomatoes

As with cheese, tomatoes are not de rigueur for first-rate pizzas, and some recipes in this book are made without tomatoes or tomato products. In Italy, as well as in my recipes, the ubiquitous canned thin pizza sauce used in most American pizzerias never appears. Instead, crushed fresh or canned tomatoes are used to impart wonderful tomato flavor.

When flavorful tomatoes are available, whether from your garden or a farmers' market, they make a wonderful topping, provided they are peeled, cut in half, and squeezed very well to eliminate as much juice as possible before slicing or chopping and arranging them on the crust. Meaty, vine-ripened tomatoes such as the Italian plum or Beefsteak varieties are the preferred choice. Most fresh tomatoes, even those labeled vine-ripened, sold in supermarkets have been developed for shipping and long storage, resulting in tasteless fruits that add very little flavor to a well-made pizza.

The finest-quality fresh tomatoes are always preferred when pizzas will be baked in blazing-hot commercial brick ovens. The lower temperature of home ovens doesn't cook tomatoes as quickly or intensely, however, resulting in a tomato topping that is not as flavorful as one produced in a wood-fired oven. In addition, slower cooking allows more of the tomato juice to seep into the crust, which can cause sogginess.

For home ovens, I generally prefer to doctor up fresh or high-quality canned tomatoes to make a thick, flavorful puree for spreading on the crust or spooning over the cheese. I've also included a recipe for a smoother sauce when tradition dictates the use of an American pizzeria–style topping. Intensely flavored sun-dried tomatoes make a good topping, too, as do oven-roasted fresh tomatoes (see page 137), a process that brings out more of their sweetness and eliminates the excess moisture that can turn even the best crust soggy.

When any sauce or moist ingredient is added to a pizza, consider reversing the common pizzeria order of the ingredients: put a layer of cheese over the dough before adding the sauce. The cheese seals the crust and helps prevent it from getting soggy from the sauce.

Olives

Although I often recommend a type of olive that is appropriate to a specific pizza, most can be used interchangeably. Brine-cured olives come packed in a light vinegar solution or olive oil. Among my favorites of this type are Greek Kalamata and French Niçoise, the latter usually packed in oil with herbs. Dry-cured olives are first packed in salt to remove most of their moisture, then they are often coated with olive oil and herbs. The black ones from Italy are perfect for pizza. Look for imported Mediterranean olives or Mediterranean-style olives from California in well-stocked supermarkets, delicatessens, or purveyors of gourmet foods. For topping pizza, avoid the bland canned black olives from California.

In Italy and France, olives are often left whole and unpitted when they are placed atop a pizza. My preference is to pit the olives when they are added to any food.

The favorite pizza topping in America is pepperoni; the least favorite is anchovy. In Europe, outside Italy, tuna is one of the most popular toppings. In Japan, sweet corn gets the most nods.

Equipment

Most kitchens include all the basics for pizza making: measuring cups and spoons, mixing bowls, and a rolling pin. Here is a list of special tools, some of which are essential and others of which are merely desirable. Most can be found at kitchen shops or restaurant-supply stores.

For Mixing

Heavy-duty stand mixer. For quick-and-easy pizza crusts, I highly recommend a heavy-duty stand mixer with a dough hook attachment. My KitchenAid never fails to produce perfect dough. With this machine, dough can be mixed, kneaded, and set aside to rise in about 10 minutes. A tip on cleanup: first rinse the bowl and beaters with cold water to loosen and remove the sticky dough, then wash them with hot soapy water. If hot water is used first, it begins to cook the dough, making it stick even more.

Bread machine. This popular home kitchen countertop appliance can be used to mix and knead pizza dough with ease.

Dough scraper. This utensil, with a flexible metal or plastic blade for prying up sticky dough from work surfaces, is essential if you knead dough by hand.

For Baking

Unglazed quarry tiles. Made of hard clay similar to that used in professional pizza ovens, quarry tiles help provide the dry, intense direct heat necessary to achieve crisp crusts in a home oven. Measure the floor of your oven, allowing for a tile-free 1-inch border for air circulation. Take the measurement with you to a ceramic-tile supplier and purchase unglazed tiles that will fill this area, having some cut to fit as needed. Look for tiles that are slightly less than 1/2 inch thick. Thicker tiles take too long to heat up, while thinner ones may crack from the intense heat. Use the tiles as directed in Preparing for Baking on page 21.

Baking stone. Numerous types of baking stones that work on the same principle as quarry tiles are available in kitchenware stores.

Averaging about 14 inches in diameter, they limit the size of the pizza and are costlier than tiles, but they are also less bulky to store and easier to install in an oven. If you decide to purchase a baking stone, keep in mind that a rectangle allows greater flexibility in pizza size and shape than a round stone.

Pizza peel. This long-handled instrument with a flat paddle-shaped foot is used by professional pizza bakers to transport the pizza to and from the hot baking surface. Wooden peels are best, although more expensive than metal ones. Both types range in size from about 10 inches to 2 feet in diameter across the paddle. Select a peel that will easily fit inside your oven and has a broad end only slightly larger than the size of the pizzas you plan to make. Measure the overall length—from handle tip to end of paddle—to make sure you will be able to turn freely in the space between your oven and the nearest obstacle. It takes practice to master the correct jerking movements for maneuvering the pizza around on the peel, so don't be discouraged if a couple of pies end up in a heap on the tiles or your kitchen floor. A rimless baking sheet can be substituted for a peel.

Pizza screens. The single most important piece of pizza baking equipment in my kitchen is the pizza screen, a round of heavy-gauge wire mesh bordered with a band of strong metal tape. Since discovering pizza screens, I have never bothered with the tedious process of transferring pizzas from a peel directly onto a tile surface or a stone, then reversing the process to retrieve the finished pie. Instead, I assemble the pizza on the screen and place the screen directly on an oven rack. The bottom of the pizza is in direct contact with the hot air circulating in the oven, so a screen-baked pizza develops a wonderfully crisp crust. And it will be even crispier if the screen is placed directly on preheated titles or a stone. Sold in restaurant-equipment outlets and well-stocked kitchenware stores, inexpensive pizza screens come in a wide variety of sizes and are easy to store. Stock up on the sizes you prefer, so you can assemble another pizza while the first one is baking. A collection of screens is great for a build-your-own pizza party.

Pizza pans. An alternative to a pizza screen is a flat ventilated pizza pan with plenty of holes that allow direct heat to reach the bottom of the crust. I do not recommend the use of old-fashioned tray pans without holes for baking pizzas, as a crust trapped inside such a pan gets too greasy and/or soggy.

Pans are essential for making deep-dish pizzas, however. Although cake pans can be used, look for deep-dish pizza pans made of heavy-gauge dark metal. They retain more heat than shiny pans do, resulting in crispier crusts. Deep-dish pans vary from 6 to 18 inches in diameter. Select one that is 1½ to 2 inches deep and heavy enough to withstand intense heat without warping. Pans with removable bottoms and springform pans make freeing of the pizza easier.

Before using a deep-dish pan for the first time, season it: wash the pan in sudsy hot water, then rinse and dry it thoroughly. Pour about 1 tablespoon vegetable oil into the pan and rub it with a sheet of paper toweling evenly over the pan bottom and sides. Place the pan in an oven preheated to 325 degrees F and heat it for about 45 minutes. Remove the pan from the oven, let it cool to room temperature, and then wipe away any excess oil with paper toweling. Rub the pan with vegetable oil each time before using. Avoid scouring the pan when cleaning, or the well-seasoned surface will be lost and crusts will stick.

Wire rack. I like to transfer pizzas directly from the oven to a rigid wire rack and let them stand for a couple of minutes to help prevent the crust from getting soggy. This also cools the pizza slightly to prevent the roof-of-the-mouth burn that commonly occurs when we can't wait for the first bite. Use the same racks sold for cooling cakes or cookies.

For Serving

Cutting tray or board. Restaurant-supply stores sell inexpensive thin metal trays made specifically for cutting and serving pizzas, although any similar tray will do. Pizzas can also be turned out onto wooden or plastic cutting boards for slicing, then transferred to a serving platter or individual plates.

Cutting implements. For flat pizzas, select a rolling wheel cutter with a good sturdy handle and protective blade guards. My choice is a heavy-duty professional pizza cutter with a metal handle and replaceable blade. For cutting calzone and other stuffed pizzas or deep-dish pizzas that are removed from their pans, choose a good-quality serrated bread knife that can also substitute for a rolling wheel cutter for slicing flat pizzas. For deep-dish pizzas that will be served directly from their pans, use a heavy-duty plastic cutting utensil, such as a pie server, to prevent cutting into the surface of the pans, as crusts may cling to cut marks in future pizzas.

Serving implements. Look for a professional chef's heavy-duty metal spatula that is wide enough to lift whole pizzas onto plates. Choose a wedge shaped serving spatula or pie server for distributing slices of large pizzas at the table.

In Italian, *pizza* means "pie," so pizza pie is redundant.

Neapolitan-Style Pizza Dough

This dough, made with only flour, yeast, water, and salt, creates a crust similar to that favored in most of Italy and by bakers of New York–style pizza. Since the flour (see page 10) used by Neapolitan bakers is softer than North American all-purpose flour, I combine 1 part plain cake flour (not self-rising) with 2 parts unbleached all-purpose flour to approximate the Italian product. Some bakers reverse the 2-to-1 ratio in favor of cake flour, while some suggest combining only 1/3 cup all-purpose flour with the balance being a fine soft flour such as imported Italian flour, cake flour, or Southern low-protein all-purpose flour. While any combination of flours yields good, yet different results, I also find that you can make an excellent Neapolitan-style crust using regular unbleached all-purpose flour on its own.

The governing body of Neapolitan bakers does not allow the addition of sugar in the crust, but if you have any doubt about the freshness of your yeast, you may wish to proof it with the aid of just a bit of sugar. To proof the yeast, add about 1/8 teaspoon sugar to the water before stirring in the yeast. This small amount of sugar will feed the yeast to prove that it is active without affecting the flavor of the dough. Let the mixture stand until foamy, 5 to 10 minutes, before adding it to the dry ingredients. Discard and start over with fresh yeast if bubbles have not formed within 10 minutes.

I generally let dough rise at room temperature because time is limited, but some pizza bakers prefer a slow overnight rise in the refrigerator to develop more flavor. Alternative directions are included if you wish to use this technique.

The customary size for pizzas in Naples is about 8 inches in diameter. To follow suit, divide the dough into 4 equal portions.

To help ensure the typical soft rim of crust common in Naples, David Rosegarten and the partners of Dean & DeLuca advocate dabbing the crust rim with a pastry brush lightly moistened with water after the pizza has baked for 3 minutes. If baking the pizza on a stone, avoid getting the water on the hot surface, which could crack it. Dampening the rim of the crust helps prevent it from getting firm and crunchy, although the latter is my preference.

1 1/4 cups warm water (110 to 115 degrees F)

2 1/4 teaspoons (1 packet or 1/4 ounce) active dry yeast

2 2/3 cups unbleached all-purpose flour

1 1/3 cups plain cake flour

2 teaspoons salt

Olive oil for brushing bowl

Pour the warm water into a small bowl. Sprinkle the yeast over the water, stir to dissolve, and set aside.

In a bowl, combine the flours and whisk to blend well.

To mix and knead the dough by hand: In a large mixing bowl, combine 3 1/2 cups of the flour with the salt. Make a well in the center of the flour mixture, then pour in the yeast mixture. Using a wooden spoon, vigorously stir the flour mixture into the well, beginning in the center and working toward the sides of the bowl, until the flour mixture is incorporated and the soft dough just begins to hold together.

Turn the dough out onto a lightly floured surface. Dust your hands with flour and knead the dough gently, pressing down on it with the heels of your hands and pushing it away from you, then partially folding it back over itself. Shift it a quarter turn and repeat the procedure. While kneading, very gradually add just enough of the remaining 1/2 cup flour until the dough is no longer too sticky; this should take about 5 minutes. As you work, use a dough scraper to pry up any bits of dough that stick to the work surface. Continue kneading until the dough is smooth, elastic, and shiny, 10 to 15 minutes longer. Knead the dough only until it feels smooth and springy but still slightly moist. Too much kneading overdevelops the gluten in the flour and results in a tough crust.

To mix and knead the dough with a food processor: In the processor bowl, combine 3½ cups of the flour with the salt and process to mix well, about 5 seconds. Add the yeast mixture and process continuously until the dough forms a single ball or several masses on top of the blade, about 30 seconds. Pinch off a piece of dough and feel it. If it is too sticky, continue processing while gradually adding just enough of the remaining ½ cup flour for the dough to lose most of its stickiness. If the dough is dry and crumbly, add warm water, a tablespoon at a time, and process until the dough is no longer too dry. Turn the dough out onto a lightly floured surface and knead by hand as described in the previous paragraph for about 2 minutes.

To mix and knead the dough with a heavy-duty stand mixer: In the mixer bowl, combine 3½ cups of the flour with the salt. Attach the flat beater and mix well at the lowest speed for about 10 seconds. Add the yeast mixture and mix well at the lowest speed for about 1 minute. Replace the flat beater with the dough hook and knead at medium speed until the dough is smooth and elastic, about 5 minutes. (After about 3 minutes, pinch off a piece of dough and feel it. If it is too sticky, continue kneading while gradually adding just enough of the remaining ½ cup flour for the dough to lose most of its stickiness. If the dough is dry and crumbly, continue kneading while gradually adding warm water, about a tablespoon at a time, until the dough is no longer too dry.)

To mix and knead the dough in a bread machine: In the mixing compartment, combine the ingredients in the order suggested in the manufacturer's manual. Run the machine as directed in the manual.

After mixing and kneading the dough by one of the preceding methods, using a pastry brush, generously grease a large bowl with oil. Shape the dough into a smooth ball by stretching the outer surface smooth and tucking the sides of the dough underneath the bottom of the ball. Place the ball, smooth top down, in the bowl, turn to coat the ball all over with oil, and rest it seam side down in the bowl. Cover the bowl tightly with plastic wrap to prevent moisture loss and set aside in a draft-free warm place for the dough to rise until doubled in bulk, about 1 hour and 10 minutes if using quick-rising yeast or about 1½ hours if using regular yeast.

Alternatively, transfer the bowl of dough to a refrigerator and let rise for 1 hour, then uncover and use your fist to punch the dough down gently to expel air. Cover tightly, return to the refrigerator, and let rise for up to 24 hours, punching down 1 or 2 more times during the rise.

When the dough has doubled in bulk, use your fist to punch it down to prevent overrising. If you cannot bake the dough risen at room temperature within 2 hours of its rising, punch the dough down again, turn it in an oiled bowl to coat once more, cover the bowl tightly with plastic wrap, and refrigerate. (The dough can be punched down a total of 4 times and kept refrigerated for up to 36 hours before the yeast is exhausted and the dough unusable.) Let chilled dough come to room temperature before proceeding.

Leave the dough whole for a large pizza, or divide it into 2 equal pieces for two pizzas, 4 equal pieces for individual pizzas, or 8 equal pieces for appetizer-sized *pizzette*. Form each piece of dough into a smooth ball in the same manner as the original large ball. If you wish to freeze dough for later use, wrap the pieces tightly in plastic wrap or seal in airtight plastic containers or freezer bags and freeze for up to 4 months. Before using, thaw in a refrigerator for 1 or 2 days or for a few hours at room temperature.

Dust the ball(s) lightly with flour and place on a lightly floured surface. If working with more than 1 ball, leave plenty of space between the balls. Cover with plastic wrap and let rise until again doubled in bulk, about 45 minutes if using quick-rising yeast or about 1 hour if using regular yeast.

Shape and bake as directed starting on page 21.

Makes enough dough for one 16-inch round pizza, two 12-inch round pizzas, four 8-inch round individual pizzas, or eight 4-inch round appetizer-sized pizzette; *for 8 servings*

California-Style Pizza Dough

Over the years, I have tried countless versions of pizza dough, yet I've never found one that I like as much as this version that I developed for my first pizza book in the 1980s. It has undergone a few refinements since then, but the basic recipe stands. The olive oil imparts a subtle flavor and richness and the crust bakes up tender yet chewy.

Alter the taste and texture of the crust by using one of the flavorful dough variations on page 20, making sure that the crust complements the toppings. The dough recipe doubles easily if you're entertaining a crowd or just want to prepare an extra batch for freezing.

If you have any doubt about the freshness of your yeast, you may wish to proof it. To proof the yeast, add about 1/8 teaspoon sugar to the water before stirring in the yeast. This small amount of sugar will feed the yeast to prove that it is active without affecting the flavor of the dough. Let the mixture stand until foamy, 5 to 10 minutes, before adding it to the dry ingredients. Discard and start over with fresh yeast if bubbles have not formed within 10 minutes.

Although I generally let dough rise at room temperature, some pizza bakers prefer a slow overnight rise in the refrigerator to develop more flavor. Alternative directions are included if you wish to use this technique.

> 1 cup warm water (110 to 115 degrees F)
> 2¼ teaspoons (1 packet or ¼ ounce)
>   active dry yeast
> About 3¼ cups unbleached all-purpose,
>   bread, or semolina flour (see
>   page 10)
> 1 teaspoon salt
> ¼ cup olive oil, preferably extra-virgin

Pour the warm water into a small bowl. Sprinkle the yeast over the water, stir to dissolve, and set aside.

To mix and knead the dough by hand: In a large mixing bowl, combine 3 cups of the flour with the salt. Make a well in the center of the flour mixture, then pour in the yeast mixture and the ¼ cup oil. Using a wooden spoon, vigorously stir the flour mixture into the well, beginning in the center and working toward the sides of the bowl, until the flour mixture is incorporated and the soft dough just begins to hold together.

Turn the dough out onto a lightly floured surface. Dust your hands with flour and knead the dough gently, pressing down on the dough with the heels of your hands and pushing it away from you, then partially folding it back over itself. Shift it a quarter turn and repeat the procedure. While kneading, very gradually add just enough of the remaining ¼ cup flour until the dough is no longer too sticky; this should take about 5 minutes. As you work, use a dough scraper to pry up any bits of dough that stick to the work surface. Continue kneading until the dough is smooth, elastic, and shiny, 10 to 15 minutes longer. Knead the dough only until it feels smooth and springy but still slightly moist. Too much kneading overdevelops the gluten in the flour and results in a tough crust.

To mix and knead the dough with a food processor: In the processor bowl, combine 3 cups of the flour with the salt and process to mix well, about 5 seconds. Add the yeast mixture and the ¼ cup oil and process continuously until the dough forms a single ball or several masses on top of the blade, about 30 seconds. Pinch off a piece of dough and feel it. If it is too sticky, continue processing while gradually adding just enough of the remaining ¼ cup flour for the dough to lose most of its stickiness. If the dough is dry and crumbly, add warm water, a tablespoon at a time, and process until the dough is no longer too dry. Turn the dough out onto a lightly floured surface and knead by hand as described in the previous paragraph for about 2 minutes.

To mix and knead the dough with a heavy-duty stand mixer: In the mixer bowl, combine 3 cups of the flour with the salt. Attach the flat beater and mix well at the lowest speed for about 10 seconds. Add the yeast mixture and the ¼ cup oil and mix well at the lowest speed for about 1 minute. Replace the flat beater with the dough hook and knead at medium speed until the dough is smooth and elastic, about 5 minutes. (After about 3 minutes, pinch off a piece of dough and feel it. If it is too sticky, continue kneading while gradually adding just enough of the remaining ¼ cup flour for the dough to lose most of its stickiness. If the dough is dry and crumbly, continue kneading while gradually adding warm water, about a tablespoon at a time, until the dough is no longer too dry.)

To mix and knead the dough in a bread machine: In the mixing compartment, combine the ingredients in the order suggested in the manufacturer's manual. Run the machine as directed in the manual.

After mixing and kneading the dough by one of the preceding methods, using a pastry brush, generously grease a large bowl with oil. Shape the dough into a smooth ball by stretching the outer surface smooth and tucking the sides of the dough underneath the bottom of the ball. Place the ball, smooth top down, in the bowl, turn to coat the ball all over with oil, and rest it seam side down in the bowl. Cover the bowl tightly with plastic wrap to prevent moisture loss and set aside in a draft-free warm place for the dough to rise until doubled in bulk, about 1 hour and 10 minutes if using quick-rising yeast or about 1½ hours if using regular yeast.

Alternatively, transfer the bowl of dough to a refrigerator and let rise for 1 hour, then uncover and use your fist to punch the dough down gently to expel air. Cover tightly, return to the refrigerator, and let rise for up to 24 hours, punching down 1 or 2 more times during the rise.

When the dough has doubled in bulk, use your fist to punch it down gently to prevent overrising. If you are using bread flour or semolina flour, turn the room temperature–risen dough in an oiled bowl to coat once more, cover the bowl tightly with plastic wrap, and set aside in a draft-free warm place until the dough is once again doubled in bulk, about 45 minutes if using quick-rising yeast or about 1 hour if using regular yeast (omit this step if using all-purpose flour). If you cannot bake the dough risen at room temperature within 2 hours of its rising, punch the dough down again, turn it in an oiled bowl to coat once more, cover the bowl tightly with plastic wrap, and refrigerate. (The dough can be punched down a total of 4 times and kept refrigerated for up to 36 hours before the yeast is exhausted and the dough unusable.) Let chilled dough come to room temperature before proceeding.

Leave the dough whole for a large pizza, or divide it into 2 equal pieces for two pizzas, 4 equal pieces for individual pizzas, or 8 equal pieces for appetizer-sized *pizzette*. Form each piece of dough into a smooth ball in the same manner as the original large ball. If you wish to freeze dough for later use, wrap the pieces tightly in plastic wrap or seal in airtight plastic containers or freezer bags and freeze for up to 4 months. Before using, thaw in a refrigerator for 1 or 2 days or for a few hours at room temperature.

Shape and bake as directed starting on page 21.

Makes enough dough for one 16-inch round pizza, two 12-inch round pizzas, four 8-inch round individual pizzas, or eight 4-inch round appetizer-sized pizzette; for 8 servings

Variations

To create crusts with a variety of flavors and textures, make the following changes to the California-Style Pizza Dough recipe. Be sure the variation complements the pizza toppings and use an oil that also complements the dough and toppings.

Cornmeal Pizza Dough. Substitute 1 cup yellow cornmeal or polenta (coarse cornmeal) for an equal amount of the flour. Stir the cornmeal, flour, and salt together before adding the yeast mixture.

Cracked Pepper Pizza Dough. Add about 3 tablespoons freshly cracked black pepper while kneading the dough.

Curried Pizza Dough. Add about 2 tablespoons high-quality curry powder along with the salt. Substitute canola or other bland vegetable oil for the olive oil.

Herbed Pizza Dough. Add about 3 tablespoons minced fresh herbs or 1 tablespoon crumbled dried herbs while kneading the dough.

Seeded Pizza Dough. Add about 1/4 cup sesame seed, lightly toasted, or 1/4 cup poppy seed while kneading the dough.

Spicy Pizza Dough. Add 2 tablespoons paprika and 1 tablespoon ground cayenne or other dried chile along with the salt.

Sweet Pizza Dough. Add 1/4 cup sugar with the flour and reduce the salt to 1/2 teaspoon. Substitute canola or other bland vegetable oil for the olive oil.

Wheat-Germ Pizza Dough. Substitute 3/4 cup wheat germ for an equal amount of the flour. Stir the wheat germ, flour, and salt together before adding the yeast mixture.

Whole-Wheat Pizza Dough. Increase the amount of warm water to 1 1/4 cups. Substitute 1 cup whole-wheat flour for an equal amount of the white flour. Stir the flours and salt together before adding the yeast mixture.

Alternative Crusts

Although nothing even comes close to the taste and texture of homemade dough, here are some quick-and-easy substitutes when time does not allow for making your own.

Commercial frozen pizza dough. Thaw in the refrigerator overnight, or at room temperature for 3 to 5 hours. Shape and bake as directed on pages 21–23.

Commercial refrigerated pizza dough. Purchase raw dough from a pizzeria. Bring to room temperature, then shape and bake as directed on pages 21–23.

Frozen bread dough. High-quality bread dough has a softer texture than pizza dough, but it can be thawed and used the same way as frozen pizza dough (see earlier entry).

Sourdough. Prepare the dough for your favorite sourdough bread recipe. Shape and bake as directed on pages 21–23.

English muffins. Split muffins. Top the cut sides and bake at 425 degrees F until the muffins are crisp.

French bread. Cut a large round or long loaf of French bread horizontally to create slices that are about 1/2 inch thick. Top and bake at 425 degrees F until the bread is crisp.

Lavosh bread. Purchase soft lavosh, not the crisp cracker version. Top and bake at 425 degrees F until the lavosh is crisp.

Nan (naan). This Indian flat bread is often available from Indian markets or restaurants. Top and bake at 425 degrees F until the nan is crisp.

Pizza crusts. Although numerous versions of prebaked pizza crusts are marketed, Boboli brand is my preference. Add toppings as directed in my recipes, then follow package directions for baking.

Tortillas. Purchase large flour tortillas used for burritos. Top and bake at 425 degrees F until the tortillas are crisp.

Preparing for Baking

While the pizza dough is rising, prepare an oven for baking.

For Pizza Other Than Deep-Dish

If baking directly on a piping-hot baking surface or on a pizza screen or ventilated pan to be placed on a hot baking surface, line an oven with unglazed quarry tiles or position a baking stone. In a gas oven, position the tiles or stone directly on the oven floor; in an electric oven, arrange the tiles or stone on the lowest rack of the oven. Preheat the prepared oven to 500 degrees F for about 30 minutes before assembling the pizza to make sure that the surface is very hot.

If baking on a pizza screen or ventilated pan without the use of tiles or a stone, position the oven racks so that the pizza will bake at the highest position. Preheat the oven to 500 degrees F while assembling the pizza.

If using a pizza screen or ventilated pan, brush it with vegetable oil or coat with cooking spray and set aside.

If baking directly on a stone or tiles, sprinkle a pizza peel with cornmeal and set aside.

Place a wire cooling rack on a countertop near the oven.

For Deep-Dish Pizza

Position the oven racks so that the pizza can be started in the lowest position, then moved to the upper part of the oven. Brush the pan with oil and set aside.

Place a wire cooling rack on a countertop near the oven.

Forming and Baking

Flat Pizzas

Shape the risen dough balls into rounds, ovals, squares, rectangles, or triangles by one of the following methods. Stretching the dough by hand works best if you enjoy a softer and chewier crust in the traditional Neapolitan style and is my preferred method for shaping pizzas. Rolling the dough produces a crust that is crispier because the rolling pin presses the air pockets out of the dough.

To shape by stretching, knead the dough for about 1 minute. Lightly flour a work surface. Shape the dough ball into a flat disk about 1 inch thick and lightly flour both sides. Starting from the center of the dough, press it out quickly with the heels of your hands, working around the dough to create the desired shape, usually a round, until the dough is about 1/2 inch thick. Dust with flour whenever needed to prevent sticking. Stop stretching before you reach the outer edge of the dough, which will form the rim of the pizza.

Rest one of your hands on the surface of the dough. Lift up a portion of the dough with your other hand and pull it gently away from the center, stretching it as thinly as possible. Continue moving around the dough, stretching it until it reaches the desired shape and size and is between 1/8 and 1/4 inch thick. If a hole forms, pinch it closed. (Be very careful when shaping the cornmeal or whole-wheat variations by this method, as those doughs tear easily.) Next, rest one of your hands near the edge of the dough and use your other hand to push the dough against it to form a slight rim, working your way completely around the perimeter of the dough.

To shape with a rolling pin, place a ball of dough on a lightly floured surface and dust the top of the dough lightly with flour. Using the heels of your hands, press the dough into a circle or other desired shape, then roll it out with a lightly floured rolling pin until it is about 1/4 inch thick, keeping the edges a little thicker than the center. While rolling the dough, pick it up and turn it over several times to stretch it. Add a little flour to the surface of the dough whenever needed to keep it from sticking. Rest one hand near the edge of the dough round and use the other hand to push the dough against it to form a slight rim around the dough, working your way completely around the perimeter of the dough.

Once the dough is shaped, lay it on the cornmeal-dusted peel or oiled screen or ventilated pan. Lightly brush the dough all over with oil as directed in individual recipes. Add the toppings as directed, leaving a 1/2-inch border around the edges. I often prefer to place the cheese on the crust before adding tomatoes or a thin sauce; the melting cheese seals the crust from the juicy toppings that can drip into the crust and make it soggy. A few recipes will direct you to prick the dough all over with a fork to prepare for a partial baking of the crust before adding fragile toppings that could burn before the crust gets done.

If using a pizza peel, before transferring the assembled pizza to the oven, give the peel a quick jerk to be sure the dough is not stuck to it. If the dough sticks, lift up one side at a time and sprinkle a bit more cornmeal underneath. Place the peel in the oven, holding the pizza over the stone or tiles, then quickly jerk the peel back 2 or 3 times, hopefully leaving the pizza centered on the cooking surface. (It takes a bit of practice, so don't be discouraged if you lose a few pizzas at first.) Bake until the crust is puffed and golden and the toppings are hot and the cheese (if using) is bubbling.

A whopping 96 percent of all Americans go out for pizza, in addition to making it at home or ordering in.

If using a pizza screen or ventilated pizza pan, place the screen or pan directly on the hot tiles or stone. If you have not lined the oven with tiles or a stone, place the screen or pan on the top rack of the preheated oven to prevent the direct heat from burning the bottom of the crust. Bake until the crust is puffed and golden and the toppings are hot and the cheese (if using) is bubbling.

It is difficult to pinpoint the actual baking time of a pizza, as it will vary according to the heat of the tiles and the oven, the thickness of the crust, and the type and amount of toppings. The way I generally make pizza, with a crust stretched to a thickness between 1/8 and 1/4 inch and a moderate amount of toppings, most are ready in about 10 minutes. Thin-crusted pizzas may be ready in about 5 minutes, while thicker ones may take up to 12 minutes, or longer. Check often after the first 5 minutes in the oven to prevent the crust from burning.

To remove a pizza from a stone or tiles, slide the peel underneath the crust. Use a metal spatula to lift a portion of the crust, if necessary, in order to slip the peel in place.

Transfer the pizza from the peel to a wire rack or place the pizza screen or pan directly on the rack and let stand for about 2 minutes to allow the crust to firm up. If placed directly on a cutting surface, steam would form, which can make the bottom of the crust limp.

To bake and serve multiple pizzas, assemble and bake as many pies at one time as the oven will accommodate; several screens are easier to work with than a single large one when baking several pies at once. Remove each pizza as soon as it is done. If you cannot serve it immediately, do not cover it with aluminum foil to keep it warm, as the crust will get soggy. If you wish to serve several pizzas at one time, consider baking them up to 1 hour ahead and, just before serving, reheat each one briefly, 2 or 3 minutes, in an oven preheated to 500 degrees F.

Calzone

Divide the dough into 4 equal pieces for individual calzone or 8 pieces for appetizer-sized *calzonetti*. Roll or stretch into rounds as directed on page 21 and brush the dough with oil as directed in recipes. Quickly arrange the fillings over one-half of each dough round, leaving a 1/2-inch border around the edges. Fold the uncovered side over the filling and press the edges of the dough together to seal. Brush the dough with oil and transfer to a cornmeal-dusted peel or a lightly oiled screen or ventilated pizza pan.

Transfer to the preheated oven and bake until the crust is crisp and golden, about 10 minutes.

Transfer the calzone or *calzonetti* from the peel to a wire rack or, if baked on a pizza screen, place the screen directly on the rack. Let stand for about 2 minutes to allow the crust to firm up.

Cookbooks of Italian recipes made no reference to pizza until the 1950s.

Deep-Dish Pizzas

To form a deep-dish crust, place a ball of dough in a well-oiled deep-dish pizza pan (see page 15). Starting in the middle, press the dough with your fingertips to cover the bottom and about 1 inch up the sides of the pan, making the dough thickness as even as possible. For a traditional crust, cover with plastic wrap or a cloth kitchen towel and let the dough rise in the pan for about 20 minutes before filling. For a thinner crust, skip the rising.

Prick the bottom of the dough every 1/2 inch with a fork, then transfer the pan to the bottom rack of a preheated oven and bake for 4 minutes. Remove the pan from the oven, brush the crust with oil, and add the toppings as directed in recipes. Return the pan to the bottom rack of the oven and bake for about 5 minutes, then move it to a rack in the upper portion of the oven and continue baking until the crust is golden and the toppings are bubbling, about 15 minutes longer.

For a stuffed deep-dish pizza, reserve one-third of the dough in the bowl. Use the larger portion to line the pan as directed above. Add the filling as directed in recipes, then roll out or stretch the reserved ball of dough to fit just inside the pan. Center it over the filling and press the edges of the crusts together to seal. Cut a 1-inch slit in the center of the top crust to allow steam to escape during cooking, then gently press the top crust down over the filling. Place the pan on the bottom rack of the preheated oven and bake for 10 minutes, then move the pan to a rack in the upper portion of the oven and bake until the crust is golden, about 15 minutes longer. When applying a tomato sauce to the top crust, add it during the final 5 minutes to avoid overcooking the sauce and creating a soggy crust. Alternatively, omit the sauce and pass it at the table.

Remove the deep-dish pan to a wire rack to cool for about 5 minutes before serving.

Grilling Pizza

My first encounter with grilled pizza was some years ago while lunching under the giant fig tree at Showley's in St. Helena, California, a favorite restaurant of Napa Valley residents. I liked the smoky nuances that grilling imparted to the pizza. Since that time, grilled pizza has become a standard item in upscale restaurants that lack wood-fired brick ovens, as well as a favorite creation of backyard grill chefs.

Almost any pizza topping can be used. If choosing meats, fish, or shellfish, however, be sure they are fully cooked before adding them. The pizzas are not on the grill long enough to cook these ingredients.

To grill a pizza, while the dough is rising, prepare a covered grill with both a hot surface area and an area that is considerably cooler. To accomplish this, arrange the hot charcoal or lava rocks (if using a gas grill) in a generous pile on one side of the fuel grate and scatter only a few on the other side. Or follow directions from your grill manufacturer for creating both direct and indirect heat.

Shape the dough as desired, keeping in mind that smaller pizzas are easier to manage on a hot grill. Place the crust on a cornmeal-dusted peel or rimless baking sheet. Place the toppings on a work surface alongside the grill. Brush the grill rack with vegetable oil, then slide the crust onto the grill rack and cook just until the bottom is set and is lightly browned, about 1 minute. If the dough begins to char or burn at any point during cooking, quickly move the crust to a cooler spot on the grill.

Remove the crust and place browned side up on a work surface. Quickly brush the browned surface with oil and add the toppings as directed in recipes. Slide the pizza onto the cooler area on the grill rack, cover, and cook, checking frequently, until the bottom of the crust is browned, the toppings are hot, and any cheese is melted, up to 6 minutes longer.

Transfer to a wire rack and let stand for about 2 minutes, then sprinkle on any garnishes, slice, and serve hot.

Serving

In restaurants in Italy, an individual-sized pizza is served to each diner, who traditionally cuts one bite at a time and eats it with a fork, or who cuts the pie into small wedges and eats the wedges out of hand. In North America, the pizza baker usually cuts a pizza into wedges and the diners pick up the wedges to eat them. If the crust is soft and the toppings moist, the first few bites of a wedge may be eaten with a fork, and then the wedge is picked up and eaten.

To serve a flat pizza, use a large spatula or rimless baking sheet to transfer the pie to a metal cutting tray or a cutting board. Lightly brush the edges of the crust with the oil suggested in the recipe to add sheen and flavor and sprinkle on any suggested finishes or garnishes. Using a rolling cutting wheel or a serrated bread knife, quickly and firmly cut all the way across the pizza in several places to form wedges. Serve sliced large pizzas directly from the cutting tray or transfer to a platter for passing at the table. Slice individual pizzas, if desired, or leave them whole, Italian style, and serve on individual plates. Individual pizzas that will be served *piadina*-style (see page 116) can be left whole or cut in half after topping and folding for sharing.

To serve a deep-dish pizza, if it was baked in a pan without a removable bottom, use a heavy-duty plastic cutting utensil to cut and serve directly from the pan. If it was baked in a pan with a removable bottom, hold the pan in the center of the bottom with one hand and use the other hand to slip off the ring carefully. If it was baked in a springform pan, unclasp and remove the ring from the pan. Using a spatula, slide the pizza from the pan bottom onto the cutting tray or board.

To serve a calzone, transfer it to a serving plate and serve immediately. If the calzone will be shared, slice across the middle into two pieces and transfer each piece to an individual serving plate.

To reheat cold or soggy pizza, unless you're like my nephew Devereux, who loves leftover pizza directly from the refrigerator, place it on a pizza screen or directly on an oven rack positioned near the top of an oven preheated to 350 degrees F. Bake until the crust is crisp and the top is bubbling, 5 to 10 minutes. Watch carefully to prevent burning the pizza.

Contemporary chefs in upscale restaurants seem to favor very thin crusts, often lacking the classic thicker rim, topped sparingly with a few simple ingredients.

Build-It-Yourself Pizza Party

One of the easiest and most enjoyable parties that I've staged through the years is held around a kitchen island where piles of ready-baked pizza crusts or balls of fresh dough and a variety of toppings await each guest's originality. If the party is small, I have bowls of risen dough ready for shaping by each participant. When the crowd is large, I purchase ready-to-top prebaked pizza crusts. There's always a stack of individual-sized pizza screens, bowls of olive oil, and several brushes on hand.

Just before the guests arrive, I set out bowls of ready-to-use toppings that I've prepared earlier in the day. These include an assortment of freshly shredded cheeses, sliced pepperoni or other meats, homemade pizza sauce, sliced ripe tomatoes, slivered roasted or sun-dried tomatoes, thinly sliced onion, minced garlic, assorted pitted olives, tapénade, pesto, sliced marinated artichoke hearts, grilled eggplant slices, assorted fresh herbs, and other favorites. In addition to the pizza fixings, I put out a big tossed salad, plenty of Zinfandel and nonalcoholic beverages, and a luscious dessert.

When everyone is ready, I quickly describe the process of making pizza and then leave my guests to their own creative devices. At one such party, it was interesting to watch a couple from Italy gingerly scatter a few carefully chosen ingredients over their crust, while some of my local friends piled on everything except the proverbial kitchen sink. It never fails that I have as much fun as my guests, and I have time to enjoy their company!

Classic
Pizzas

Whether they come from Naples, other parts of Italy, or the New World, the traditional pizzas included in this section have withstood the test of time to become true classics of the pizza bakers' art.

27

Neapolitan-Style Pizza Dough
   (page 16)
Seasoned Tomato Pulp (page 136)
Vegetable oil or cooking spray for
   greasing pizza screen or
   ventilated pizza pan (if using)
Cornmeal for sprinkling pizza peel
   (if using)
Extra-virgin olive oil for brushing
   crust and drizzling over
   toppings
2 teaspoons thinly sliced garlic, or
   to taste
1 tablespoon chopped fresh oregano,
   or 1 teaspoon crumbled dried
   oregano
Salt

Tomato and Garlic Pizza (Pizza Marinara)

Naples deserves the credit for inventing pizza as we know it, and that port city still produces some of the best versions you'll ever eat. The Association of Verace Pizza Napoletana, the organization dedicated to the protection and promotion of the authentic Neapolitan pizza, dictates that the dough for *pizza marinara*, also known to many as *pizza alla napoletana* outside its home city, must contain only flour, salt, yeast, and water, and the basic toppings are limited to tomatoes, olive oil, oregano, and garlic. Neapolitan pizza bakers, however, often add a variety of additional toppings to create pizzas that are each known by different names. To follow suit, scatter anchovy fillets, sliced mushrooms or sweet peppers, onion rings, capers, olives, crushed dried chile, or chopped prosciutto, ham, or salami over the tomatoes. Just be sure to avoid a complicated combination of too many ingredients, and as the pizza association of Naples directs, be sure the toppings "are not in contrast with the rules of gastronomy."

Neapolitan pizzas are not made with the smooth tomato sauce, used in most American pizzerias, but with crushed tomatoes. Since great-tasting tomatoes are only available for a short time in the summer through early fall, I prefer to "doctor" fresh or canned tomatoes. If you have flavorful ripe tomatoes on hand during the peak of tomato season, peel, seed, drain, and finely chop enough to use as an alternative to the prepared pulp.

If necessary, review Making Perfect Pizza at Home (pages 9–25).

Make the Neapolitan-Style Pizza Dough and set aside to rise as directed.

Prepare the Seasoned Tomato Pulp as directed and set aside to cool to room temperature.

About 30 minutes before baking the pizza, prepare an oven as directed on page 21 and preheat it to 500 degrees F. If using a pizza screen or ventilated pan, brush it with vegetable oil or coat with spray and set aside. If baking directly on a stone or tiles, sprinkle a pizza peel with cornmeal and set aside.

On a lightly floured surface, roll out or stretch the dough and shape it as desired. Place the dough on the prepared screen, pan, or peel. Brush the dough all over with olive oil, then top with the tomato, leaving a ½-inch border around the edges. Sprinkle with the garlic, oregano, and salt to taste, and drizzle with olive oil. If using a pizza peel, give it a quick, short jerk to be sure that the bottom of the crust has not stuck to it.

Transfer the pizza to the preheated oven and bake until the crust is golden, about 10 minutes.

Remove the pizza to a wire rack and let stand for about 2 minutes, then transfer to a cutting tray or board and lightly brush the edges of the crust with olive oil. Slice and serve immediately.

Makes 8 servings

Neapolitan-Style Pizza Dough
    (page 16)
Vegetable oil or cooking spray for
    greasing pizza screen or
    ventilated pizza pan (if using)
Cornmeal for sprinkling pizza peel
    (if using)
Extra-virgin olive oil for brushing
    crust
2 tablespoons very thinly sliced
    garlic
1½ tablespoons chopped fresh
    oregano, or 1½ teaspoons
    crumbled dried oregano
Salt
Crushed dried chile

Garlic and Olive Oil Pizza (Pizza Aglio e Olio)

This simple pie of Naples is reminiscent of the ancient predecessors of the modern pizza that were enjoyed for centuries before the introduction of cheese or tomatoes to the Italian diet. A pizza prepared without tomatoes is also known as a *pizza bianca* (see page 32).
    If desired, lightly sprinkle the hot pizza with freshly grated Parmigiano-Reggiano cheese.

If necessary, review Making Perfect Pizza at Home (pages 9–25).

Make the Neapolitan-Style Pizza Dough and set aside to rise as directed.

About 30 minutes before baking the pizza, prepare an oven as directed on page 21 and preheat it to 500 degrees F. If using a pizza screen or ventilated pan, brush it with vegetable oil or coat with spray and set aside. If baking directly on a stone or tiles, sprinkle a pizza peel with cornmeal and set aside.

On a lightly floured surface, roll out or stretch the dough and shape it as desired. Place the dough on the prepared screen, pan, or peel. Brush the dough all over with olive oil, then sprinkle with the garlic and oregano, leaving a ½-inch border around the edges. Sprinkle with salt and chile to taste. If using a pizza peel, give it a quick, short jerk to be sure that the bottom of the crust has not stuck to it.

Transfer the pizza to the preheated oven and bake until the crust is golden, about 10 minutes.

Remove the pizza to a wire rack and let stand for about 2 minutes, then transfer to a cutting tray or board and lightly brush the edges of the crust with olive oil. Slice and serve immediately.

Makes 8 servings

2 cups Roasted Tomatoes (page 137)

Neapolitan-Style Pizza Dough (page 16) or California-Style Pizza Dough (page 18)

Vegetable oil or cooking spray for greasing pizza screen or ventilated pizza pan (if using)

Cornmeal for sprinkling pizza peel (if using)

Extra-virgin olive oil for brushing crust and drizzling over toppings

1 tablespoon minced garlic, or to taste

Salt

1/4 cup freshly grated Parmesan cheese (about 1 ounce), preferably Parmigiano-Reggiano

About 24 whole fresh basil leaves, or 1/2 cup shredded or chopped fresh basil

Tomato Basil Pizza (Pizza con Pomodoro e Basilico)

For many summers I topped this pizza with sliced fresh tomatoes, always making certain that they were vine-ripened and flavorful. I put that rendition on the cover of my first pizza cookbook, but I've since discovered that I prefer using intensely flavored roasted tomatoes. You may still choose to use fresh tomatoes, but be sure to squeeze and drain off as much juice as possible to prevent a soggy crust. Alternatively, use Seasoned Tomato Pulp (page 136).

If necessary, review Making Perfect Pizza at Home (pages 8-25).

Prepare the Roasted Tomatoes as directed, slice or chop coarsely, and set aside to cool to room temperature.

Make the selected pizza dough and set aside to rise as directed.

About 30 minutes before baking the pizza, prepare an oven as directed on page 21 and preheat it to 500 degrees F. If using a pizza screen or ventilated pan, brush it with vegetable oil or coat it with spray and set aside. If baking directly on a stone or tiles, sprinkle a pizza peel with cornmeal and set aside.

On a lightly floured surface, roll out or stretch the dough and shape it as desired. Place the dough on the prepared screen, pan, or peel. Brush the dough all over with olive oil. Sprinkle the garlic over the dough, then top with the tomatoes, leaving a 1/2-inch border around the edges. Sprinkle with salt to taste and drizzle with olive oil. If using a pizza peel, give it a quick, short jerk to be

sure that the bottom of the crust has not stuck to it.

Transfer the pizza to the preheated oven and bake until the crust is golden, about 10 minutes.

Remove the pizza to a wire rack and let stand for about 2 minutes, then transfer to a cutting tray or board and lightly brush the edges of the crust with olive oil. Sprinkle with the Parmesan cheese and basil. Slice and serve immediately.

Makes 6 servings

Neapolitan-Style Pizza Dough
(page 16)

Seasoned Tomato Pulp (page 136), or 2 cups peeled, seeded, well-drained, and finely chopped ripe tomato (see page 12)

Vegetable oil or cooking spray for greasing pizza screen or ventilated pizza pan (if using)

Cornmeal for sprinkling pizza peel (if using)

Extra-virgin olive oil for brushing crust and drizzling over toppings

8 ounces fresh mozzarella cheese packed in water, preferably water-buffalo type from Italy, thinly sliced and cut into small pieces, or 3 cups freshly shredded high-quality semisoft mozzarella cheese (about 9 ounces), preferably made with whole milk

½ cup freshly grated Parmesan cheese (about 2 ounces), preferably Parmigiano-Reggiano

Salt

About 8 large fresh basil leaves

Tomato, Mozzarella, and Basil Pizza (Pizza Margherita)

Italy's nineteenth-century Queen Margherita adored this pizza, which prompted Raffaele Esposito, who baked it for her, to name it in her honor (see page 6). Today, the simple combination of ingredients that captures the colors of the Italian flag is arguably the world's most popular pizza presentation. When made with tomatoes and basil at the peak of their season, fresh mozzarella, fruity extra-virgin olive oil, and the finest Parmesan, this pie has no rival.

Choose fresh tomatoes only when they are at their peak. At other times, use the Seasoned Tomato Pulp, which approximates the flavor of ripe tomatoes that have been exposed to the blistering heat of a wood-burning oven.

If necessary, review Making Perfect Pizza at Home (pages 9–25).

Make the Neapolitan-Style Pizza Dough and set aside to rise as directed.

If using Seasoned Tomato Pulp, prepare as directed and set aside to cool to room temperature. If using fresh tomato, reserve for later use.

About 30 minutes before baking the pizza, prepare an oven as directed on page 21 and preheat it to 500 degrees F. If using a pizza screen or ventilated pan, brush it with vegetable oil or coat with spray and set aside. If baking directly on a stone or tiles, sprinkle a pizza peel with cornmeal and set aside.

On a lightly floured surface, roll out or stretch the dough and shape it as desired. Place the dough on the prepared screen, pan, or peel. Brush the dough all over with olive oil, then top with the tomato, leaving a ½-inch border around the edges. Layer the mozzarella cheese over the tomato, sprinkle with ¼ cup of the Parmesan cheese and salt to taste, and drizzle with olive oil. If using a pizza peel, give it a quick, short jerk to be sure that the bottom of the crust has not stuck to it.

Transfer the pizza to the preheated oven and bake until the crust is golden, about 10 minutes.

Remove the pizza to a wire rack and let stand for about 2 minutes, then transfer to a cutting tray or board and lightly brush the edges of the crust with olive oil. Sprinkle with the remaining ¼ cup Parmesan cheese. Tear the basil leaves into small pieces and scatter over the pizza. Slice and serve immediately.

Makes 8 servings

Neapolitan-Style Pizza Dough
(page 16)

Vegetable oil or cooking spray for
greasing pizza screen or
ventilated pizza pan (if using)

Cornmeal for sprinkling pizza peel
(if using)

Extra-virgin olive oil for brushing
crust and drizzling over
toppings

2 teaspoons minced garlic

8 ounces fresh soft mozzarella
cheese packed in water, preferably water-buffalo type from
Italy, thinly sliced and cut into
small pieces, or 3 cups freshly
shredded high-quality semisoft
mozzarella cheese (about 9
ounces), preferably made with
whole milk

1/2 cup freshly grated Parmesan
cheese (about 2 ounces),
preferably Parmigiano-
Reggiano

Salt

White Pizza
(Pizza Bianca)

When prepared without tomatoes, Italian pizza is dubbed *bianca*. Additional toppings often include onions, potatoes, and other white vegetables, as well as anchovies, capers, olives, and minced fresh herbs. Pair the pizza with a glass of buttery Chardonnay.

If necessary, review Making Perfect Pizza at Home (pages 9–25).

Make the Neapolitan-Style Pizza Dough and set aside to rise as directed.

About 30 minutes before baking the pizza, pre-pare an oven as directed on page 21 and preheat it to 500 degrees F. If using a pizza screen or ven-tilated pan, brush it with vegetable oil or coat with spray and set aside. If baking directly on a stone or tiles, sprinkle a pizza peel with cornmeal and set aside.

On a lightly floured surface, roll out or stretch the dough and shape it as desired. Place the dough on the prepared screen, pan, or peel. Brush the dough all over with olive oil, then sprinkle with the garlic, leaving a 1/2-inch border around the edges. Top with the mozzarella cheese, sprinkle with 1/4 cup of the Parmesan cheese and salt to taste, and drizzle with olive oil. If using a pizza peel, give it a quick, short jerk to be sure that the bottom of the crust has not stuck to it.

Transfer the pizza to the preheated oven and bake until the crust is golden, about 10 minutes.

Remove the pizza to a wire rack and let stand for about 2 minutes, then transfer to a cutting tray or board and lightly brush the edges of the crust with olive oil. Sprinkle with the remaining 1/4 cup Parmesan cheese. Slice and serve immediately.

Makes 8 servings

Neapolitan-Style Pizza Dough (page 16) or California-Style Pizza Dough (page 18)

1 cup freshly shredded high-quality semisoft mozzarella cheese (about 3 ounces), preferably made with whole milk

1 cup freshly shredded Italian Fontina cheese (about 5 ounces)

1/2 cup crumbled Gorgonzola cheese (about 2 ounces)

1/2 cup freshly grated Parmesan cheese (about 2 ounces), preferably Parmigiano-Reggiano

Vegetable oil or cooking spray for greasing pizza screen or ventilated pizza pan (if using)

Cornmeal for sprinkling pizza peel (if using)

Extra-virgin olive oil for brushing crust and drizzling over toppings

Salt

Freshly ground black pepper

Four Cheese Pizza (Pizza Quattro Formaggi)

Four Italian cheeses melt together atop this simply sublime pizza. Vary the idea with your favorite good-melting cheeses, adding a shower of fresh or dried herbs and/or minced garlic. For a tomato and cheese pie, scatter finely chopped well-drained ripe tomatoes, Roasted Tomatoes (page 137), or drained sun-dried tomatoes packed in olive oil over the cheese.

If necessary, review Making Perfect Pizza at Home (pages 9–25).

Make the selected pizza dough and set aside to rise as directed.

In a bowl, combine the mozzarella, Fontina, Gorgonzola, and Parmesan cheeses and set aside.

About 30 minutes before baking the pizza, prepare an oven as directed on page 21 and preheat it to 500 degrees F. If using a pizza screen or ventilated pan, brush it with vegetable oil or coat with spray and set aside. If baking directly on a stone or tiles, sprinkle a pizza peel with cornmeal and set aside.

On a lightly floured surface, roll out or stretch the dough and shape it as desired. Place the dough on the prepared screen, pan, or peel. Brush the dough all over with olive oil, then top with the cheese mixture, leaving a 1/2-inch border around the edges. Sprinkle with salt and pepper to taste and drizzle evenly with olive oil. If using a pizza peel, give it a quick, short jerk to be sure that the bottom of the crust has not stuck to it.

Transfer the pizza to the preheated oven and bake until the crust is golden, about 10 minutes.

Remove the pizza to a wire rack and let stand for about 2 minutes, then transfer to a cutting tray or board and lightly brush the edges of the crust with olive oil. Slice and serve immediately.

Makes 8 servings

Neapolitan-Style Pizza Dough
(page 16)

Seasoned Tomato Pulp (page 136), or
2 cups peeled, seeded, well-
drained, and finely chopped
ripe tomato (see page 12)

Vegetable oil or cooking spray for
greasing pizza screen or
ventilated pizza pan (if using)

Cornmeal for sprinkling pizza peel
(if using)

Extra-virgin olive oil for brushing
crust and drizzling over
toppings

8 ounces fresh soft mozzarella
cheese packed in water, preferably water-buffalo type from
Italy, thinly sliced and cut into
small pieces, or 3 cups freshly
shredded high-quality semisoft
mozzarella cheese (about 9
ounces), preferably made with
whole milk

8 flat anchovy fillets, coarsely
chopped

1/4 cup coarsely chopped, pitted dry-
cured black olives, preferably
from Italy

2 tablespoons drained small capers

1/2 cup freshly grated Parmesan
cheese (about 2 ounces),
preferably Parmigiano-
Reggiano

Salt

Crushed dried chile

Spicy Tomato and Cheese Pizza with Anchovies, Olives, and Capers (Pizza Vesuvio)

Be generous with the crushed chile to give this traditional Neapolitan pizza plenty of heat in homage to the tempestuous nature and incendiary cone of the nearby volcano.

If necessary, review Making Perfect Pizza at Home (pages 9–25).

Make the Neapolitan-Style Pizza Dough and set aside to rise as directed.

If using Seasoned Tomato Pulp, prepare as direct-ed and set aside to cool to room temperature. If using fresh tomato, reserve for later use.

About 30 minutes before baking the pizza, pre-pare an oven as directed on page 21 and preheat it to 500 degrees F. If using a pizza screen or ven-tilated pan, brush it with vegetable oil or coat with spray and set aside. If baking directly on a stone or tiles, sprinkle a pizza peel with cornmeal and set aside.

On a lightly floured surface, roll out or stretch the dough and shape it as desired. Place the dough on the prepared screen, pan, or peel. Brush the dough all over with olive oil, then top with the tomato, leaving a 1/2-inch border around the edges. Layer the mozzarella cheese over the tomato and scatter the anchovy fillets, olives, and capers over the cheese. Sprinkle with 1/4 cup of the Parmesan cheese and salt and crushed chile

to taste, then drizzle with olive oil. If using a pizza peel, give it a quick, short jerk to be sure that the bottom of the crust has not stuck to it.

Transfer the pizza to the preheated oven and bake until the crust is golden, about 10 minutes.

Remove the pizza to a wire rack and let stand for about 2 minutes, then transfer to a cutting tray or board and lightly brush the edges of the crust with olive oil. Sprinkle with the remaining 1/4 cup Parmesan cheese. Slice and serve immediately.

Makes 8 servings

Neapolitan-Style Pizza Dough
(page 16)

About 2 cups fresh small arugula
leaves

Seasoned Tomato Pulp (page 136),
or 2 cups peeled, seeded, well-
drained, and finely chopped
ripe tomato (see page 12)

Vegetable oil or cooking spray for
greasing pizza screen or ventilated pizza pan (if using)

Cornmeal for sprinkling pizza peel
(if using)

Extra-virgin olive oil for brushing
crust and drizzling over
toppings

8 ounces fresh soft mozzarella
cheese packed in water,
preferably water-buffalo type
from Italy, thinly sliced and cut
into small pieces, or 3 cups
freshly shredded high-quality
semisoft mozzarella cheese
(about 9 ounces), preferably
made with whole milk

1/2 cup freshly grated Parmesan
cheese (about 2 ounces),
preferably Parmigiano-
Reggiano

Salt

8 thin slices high-quality prosciutto,
preferably from Italy, cut into
bite-sized pieces

Be sure to use arugula, also known as rocket cress or roquette, that is tender and peppery tasting. Look for the best prosciutto, Italian salt-cured and air-dried ham, that you can find. Although versions are made in the United States, the best-tasting prosciutto is imported and labeled according to its Italian origin, such as *prosciutto di Parma*.

If necessary, review Making Perfect Pizza at Home (pages 9–25).

Make the Neapolitan-Style Pizza Dough and set aside to rise as directed.

Wash the arugula under cold running water. Place in a salad spinner and spin to remove as much water as possible. Pat dry with paper toweling. Wrap in a cloth kitchen towel or paper toweling and refrigerate for at least 30 minutes to crisp, or place the wrapped leaves in a plastic bag and refrigerate for up to several hours.

If using Seasoned Tomato Pulp, prepare as directed and set aside to cool to room temperature. If using fresh tomatoes, reserve for later use.

About 30 minutes before baking the pizza, prepare an oven as directed on page 21 and preheat it to 500 degrees F. If using a pizza screen or ventilated pan, brush it with vegetable oil or coat with spray and set aside. If baking directly on a stone or tiles, sprinkle a pizza peel with cornmeal and set aside.

On a lightly floured surface, roll out or stretch the dough and shape it as desired. Place the dough on the prepared screen, pan, or peel. Brush the dough all over with olive oil, then top with the tomato, leaving a 1/2-inch border around the edges. Layer the mozzarella cheese over the tomato, sprinkle with 1/4 cup of the Parmesan cheese and salt to taste, and drizzle with olive oil. If using a pizza peel, give it a quick, short jerk to be sure that the bottom of the crust has not stuck to it.

Transfer the pizza to the preheated oven and bake until the crust is golden, about 10 minutes.

Remove the pizza to a wire rack and let stand for about 2 minutes, then transfer to a cutting tray or board and lightly brush the edges of the crust with olive oil. Scatter the arugula over the pizza and scatter the prosciutto pieces over the top. Sprinkle with the remaining 1/4 cup Parmesan cheese. Slice and serve immediately.

Makes 8 servings

½ cup Roasted Tomatoes (page 137),
    or 1 cup peeled, seeded,
    well-drained, and chopped ripe
    tomato (see page 12)
Neapolitan-Style Pizza Dough
    (page 16)
2 tablespoons olive oil
1¼ cups thinly sliced fresh
    mushrooms
Salt
Freshly ground black pepper
Vegetable oil or cooking spray for
    greasing pizza screen or
    ventilated pizza pan (if using)
Cornmeal for sprinkling pizza peel
    (if using)
Extra-virgin olive oil for brushing
    crust and drizzling over
    toppings
2 teaspoons minced garlic
¼ cup freshly grated Parmesan
    cheese (about 1 ounce), prefer-
    ably Parmigiano-Reggiano
6 ounces thinly sliced high-quality
    prosciutto, preferably from Italy
4 ounces fresh soft mozzarella
    cheese packed in water, prefer-
    ably water-buffalo type from
    Italy, thinly sliced and cut into
    small pieces, or 1½ cups
    freshly shredded high-quality
    semisoft mozzarella cheese
    (about 4½ ounces), preferably
    made with whole milk
¾ cup chopped, well-drained fresh
    or canned clams or mussels
Salt
1 tablespoon minced fresh oregano
1 tablespoon shredded fresh basil

1 tablespoon minced fresh flat-leaf
    parsley
1 tablespoon minced fresh thyme
Crushed dried chile for serving
Freshly grated Parmesan cheese,
    preferably Parmigiano-
    Reggiano, for serving

Four Seasons Pizza (Pizza Quattro Stagioni)

The crust of this traditional pie is divided into four sections, each topped by separate ingredients to represent the subtle changing of the seasons in southern Italy. Use the idea and vary the toppings to celebrate your own area's seasonal bounty or favorite pizza toppings.

If using Roasted Tomatoes, prepare as directed, chop coarsely, and set aside to cool to room temperature. If using fresh tomato, reserve for later use.

If necessary, review Making Perfect Pizza at Home (pages 9–25).

Make the Neapolitan-Style Pizza Dough and set aside to rise as directed.

In a sauté pan or skillet, heat the 2 tablespoons olive oil over medium-high heat. Add the mushrooms and cook, stirring frequently, until tender, 3 to 4 minutes. Season to taste with salt and pepper, transfer to a bowl, and set aside.

About 30 minutes before baking the pizza, prepare an oven as directed on page 21 and preheat it to 500 degrees F. If using a pizza screen or ventilated pan, brush it with vegetable oil or coat with spray and set aside. If baking directly on a stone or tiles, sprinkle a pizza peel with cornmeal and set aside.

Reserve one-fourth of the dough. On a lightly floured surface, roll out or stretch the remaining dough and shape it into a 14-inch round. Place the dough on the prepared screen, pan, or peel. Divide the reserved dough into 2 pieces. Using the palms of your hands, roll each piece into a ball and then into a cylinder about 20 inches long and ⅓ inch in diameter. Holding each cylinder at each end, twist in opposite directions to resemble a rope. Place the 2 cylinders at right angles across the pizza crust to form even quarters and trim off any extra dough from each end. Brush the dough all over with olive oil.

Sprinkle all the quarter sections of the dough with the garlic, leaving the dough ropes exposed and a ½-inch border around the outer rim. Sprinkle one section with the Parmesan cheese, then top with the prosciutto. Fill another section with the mozzarella cheese and top it with half of the tomatoes. Fill the third section with the clams or mussels. In the final section, combine the mushrooms and remaining tomatoes. Sprinkle all of the toppings with salt to taste and drizzle with olive oil. If using a pizza peel, give it a quick, short jerk to be sure that the bottom of the crust has not stuck to it.

Transfer the pizza to the preheated oven and bake until the crust is golden, about 10 minutes.

Remove the pizza to a wire rack and let stand for about 2 minutes, then transfer to a cutting tray or board and lightly brush the edges and cross pieces of the crust with olive oil. Sprinkle the minced oregano over the prosciutto, the shredded basil over the mozzarella-tomato section, the minced parsley over the clams or mussels, and the thyme over the mushroom-tomato mixture. Slice and serve immediately. Offer chile and Parmesan at the table for sprinkling over the pizza.

Makes 8 servings

California-Style Pizza Dough (page 18) or Neapolitan-Style Pizza Dough (page 16)

¼ cup olive oil

3 pounds yellow or white onions, thinly sliced

1 tablespoon minced garlic

1 tablespoon minced fresh marjoram, or 1 teaspoon crumbled dried marjoram

1 tablespoon minced fresh thyme, or 1 teaspoon crumbled dried thyme

1½ teaspoons minced fresh rosemary, or ½ teaspoon crumbled dried rosemary

Salt

Freshly ground black pepper

Vegetable oil or cooking spray for greasing pizza screen or ventilated pizza pan (if using)

Cornmeal for sprinkling pizza peel (if using)

Extra-virgin olive oil for brushing crust

12 flat anchovy fillets

1 cup drained, pitted Niçoise olives or other flavorful olives (see recipe introduction)

1 tablespoon drained small capers

1½ tablespoons pine nuts

½ small lemon, sliced paper-thin, then each slice cut into 4 wedges (optional)

Minced fresh flat-leaf parsley for garnish

Provençal Caramelized Onion Pizza (Pissaladière)

Traditionally, the crust for this specialty of Nice is formed into a rectangle. The addition of lemon is an idea that I gleaned from Absinthe Brasserie in San Francisco. It gives the caramelized onion topping an appealing piquancy. For good caramelization, choose onions that are somewhat dry. Freshly picked onions contain a lot of water, which makes them fall apart before they achieve good color.

The name for this pizza comes from the French *pissala*, a classic condiment made from anchovies and olives, two of the major elements in this pie. The olives of choice for this preparation are imported brine-cured purplish Niçoise olives packed with herbs in olive oil from Provence. Alternate choices include black wrinkled dry-cured olives from Italy or flavorful brine-cured olives from other Mediterranean countries or California. Avoid the bland canned "ripe" olives on supermarket shelves. In France the olives are left unpitted, which look great atop a *pissaladière,* but I prefer offering it with pitted olives.

If necessary, review Making Perfect Pizza at Home (pages 9–25).

Make the selected pizza dough and set aside to rise as directed.

In a large, heavy pan, heat the ¼ cup olive oil over medium heat. Add the onions and garlic and toss well to coat with the oil. Stir in the marjoram, thyme, and rosemary and sprinkle generously with salt and pepper. Cover, reduce the heat to medium-low, and cook, stirring occasionally, until the onions are soft and lightly colored, about 30 minutes. Uncover, increase the heat to medium, and cook, stirring frequently, until the onions are very tender and well caramelized, 25 minutes or longer, depending on the moisture content of the onions. Remove from the heat and set aside to cool to room temperature.

About 30 minutes before baking the pizza, prepare an oven as directed on page 21 and preheat it to 500 degrees F. If using a pizza screen or ventilated pan, brush it with vegetable oil or coat with spray and set aside. If baking directly on a stone or tiles, sprinkle a pizza peel with cornmeal and set aside.

On a lightly floured surface, roll out or stretch the dough into a large rectangle or other shape as desired. Place the dough on the prepared screen, pan, or peel. Brush the dough all over with olive oil, then top with the caramelized onions, leaving a ½-inch border around the edges. Arrange the anchovy fillets on top and then scatter the olives, capers, pine nuts, and lemon wedges (if using) over the onions. If using a pizza peel, give it a quick, short jerk to be sure that the bottom of the crust has not stuck to it.

▶

Saturday night is the biggest night of the week for eating pizza.

Transfer the pizza to the preheated oven and bake until the crust is golden, about 10 minutes.

Remove the pizza to a wire rack and let stand for about 2 minutes, then transfer to a cutting tray or board and lightly brush the edges of the crust with olive oil. Sprinkle with parsley. Slice and serve immediately.

Makes 8 servings

Variation
For a tomato *pissaladière,* omit the caramelized onions and generously spread the crust with 2 cups Seasoned Tomato Pulp (page 136).

Neapolitan-Style Pizza Dough
(page 16)
Seasoned Tomato Pulp (page 136)
Vegetable oil or cooking spray for
greasing pizza screen or
ventilated pizza pan (if using)
Cornmeal for sprinkling pizza peel
(if using)
Extra-virgin olive oil for brushing
crust and drizzling over
toppings
2 tablespoons minced fresh
oregano, or 2 teaspoons
crumbled dried oregano
3 cups crumbled high-quality feta
cheese (about 12 ounces)
1 cup drained, pitted Kalamata olives
1 cup sliced pickled peppers
(peperoncini)
1 cup chopped red onion
2 tablespoons drained small capers
½ cup freshly grated kasseri cheese
(about 2 ounces)

Greek-Style Pizza

Although Italy gets most of the credit for giving pizza to the world, it was the Greeks who brought the idea for seasoned flat bread to southern Italy. The toppings on this pizza are typical of those offered by street vendors in Greece.

Look for eggplant-hued Kalamata olives, chartreuse pickled peppers, and other Greek ingredients in well-stocked supermarkets or grocers that cater to Greek-Americans. If you can't locate Greek kasseri, a goat's or sheep's milk grating cheese, substitute a domestic version or Italian pecorino-romano or Parmesan.

If necessary, review Making Perfect Pizza at Home (pages 9–25).

Make the Neapolitan-Style Pizza Dough and set aside to rise as directed.

Prepare the Seasoned Tomato Pulp as directed and set aside to cool to room temperature.

About 30 minutes before baking the pizza, prepare an oven as directed on page 21 and preheat it to 500 degrees F. If using a pizza screen or ventilated pan, brush it with vegetable oil or coat with spray and set aside. If baking directly on a stone or tiles, sprinkle a pizza peel with cornmeal and set aside.

On a lightly floured surface, roll out or stretch the dough and shape it as desired. Place the dough on the prepared screen, pan, or peel. Brush the dough all over with olive oil, then top with the tomato pulp, leaving a ½-inch border around the edges. Sprinkle the oregano over the tomato layer, then top with the feta cheese. Scatter the olives, peppers, onion, and capers over the cheese and drizzle with olive oil. If using a pizza peel, give it a quick, short jerk to be sure that the bottom of the crust has not stuck to it.

Transfer the pizza to the preheated oven and bake until the crust is golden, about 10 minutes.

Remove the pizza to a wire rack and let stand for about 2 minutes, then transfer to a cutting tray or board and lightly brush the edges of the crust with olive oil. Sprinkle with the kasseri cheese. Slice and serve immediately.

Makes 8 servings

Neapolitan-Style Pizza Dough
   (page 16)
2 tablespoons olive oil
1 cup finely chopped white or yellow
   onion
1 cup finely chopped red sweet
   pepper
1 pound finely minced or ground
   lean lamb
2 cups peeled, seeded, well-drained,
   and finely chopped ripe or
   canned tomato
2 tablespoons tomato paste
1 tablespoon pomegranate molasses
   (optional)
3/4 teaspoon crushed dried chile, or
   to taste
1 1/2 teaspoons ground allspice
1/2 teaspoon ground cumin
1/2 cup minced fresh flat-leaf parsley
Salt
Freshly ground black pepper
About 1 tablespoon freshly squeezed
   lemon juice (if not using
   pomegranate molasses)
Vegetable oil or cooking spray for
   greasing pizza screen or
   ventilated pizza pan (if using)
Cornmeal for sprinkling pizza peel
   (if using)
Olive oil for brushing crust
1/2 cup finely chopped red onion
Plain yogurt, lightly whisked, for
   serving

Turkish Lamb "Pizza" (Pide Lahmajun)

Popular throughout the Middle East, where they're known by a variety of similar names, these pies are cooked only until the crust is done but not crisp. The piping-hot pies are rolled up and eaten out of hand, sometimes enveloped in a waxed-paper wrapper in the style of a gyro sandwich. If desired, the hot "pizza" can be showered with crumbled feta cheese, chopped grilled eggplant, chopped cucumber, sliced ripe tomatoes, or toasted pine nuts before rolling.

If necessary, review Making Perfect Pizza at Home (pages 9–25).

Make the Neapolitan-Style Pizza Dough and set aside to rise as directed.

In a heavy sauté pan or skillet, heat the 2 tablespoons olive oil over medium-high heat. Add the white or yellow onion and sweet pepper and cook, stirring frequently, until soft but not browned, about 5 minutes. Add the lamb and cook, stirring constantly and breaking up the meat with a spoon, until the meat is just past the pink stage, about 3 minutes. Stir in the chopped tomato, tomato paste, pomegranate molasses (if using), chile, allspice, cumin, and 1/4 cup of the minced parsley. Reduce the heat to medium and cook, stirring frequently, until the mixture is almost dry, 5 to 10 minutes. Season to taste with salt, pepper, and lemon juice (if not using pomegranate molasses) and set aside to cool completely.

About 30 minutes before baking the pizza, prepare an oven as directed on page 21 and preheat it to 500 degrees F. If using a pizza screen or ventilated pan, brush it with vegetable oil or coat with spray and set aside. If baking directly on a stone or tiles, sprinkle a pizza peel with cornmeal and set aside.

Divide the dough into 8 equal pieces and form each into a ball. Cover loosely with plastic wrap to keep the dough from drying out.

Working with 1 dough ball at a time, on a lightly floured surface, roll out or stretch the dough into a round about 1/8 inch thick and 7 to 8 inches in diameter. Place the dough on the prepared screen, pan, or peel. Brush the dough all over with olive oil, then top with about 1/2 cup of the lamb mixture, spreading it all the way to the edges of the dough. Repeat with the remaining balls of dough to form as many pizzas as will fit into the oven at one time without crowding. If using a pizza peel, give it a quick, short jerk to be sure that the bottom of each crust has not stuck to it.

Transfer the pizzas to the preheated oven and bake until the crusts are done but only tinged with brown and are still soft and pliable, about 5 minutes.

Remove the pizzas to a work surface, sprinkle with some of the red onion and remaining parsley, and drizzle with a little yogurt. Roll each pizza into a cylinder and serve immediately.

Makes 8 servings

Cornmeal Pizza Dough (page 20)
Seasoned Tomato Pulp (page 136),
    or 1 cup Pizzeria-Style Tomato
    Sauce (page 138)
Extra-virgin olive oil for brushing pan
    and crust and drizzling over
    toppings
3 cups freshly shredded high-quality
    semisoft mozzarella cheese
    (about 9 ounces), preferably
    made with whole milk
½ cup freshly grated Parmesan
    cheese (about 2 ounces),
    preferably Parmigiano-
    Reggiano
12 ounces lean sweet or hot Italian
    sausage, removed from
    casings and crumbled
2 tablespoons chopped fresh flat-
    leaf parsley

Deep-Dish Sausage Pizza, Chicago Style

One of Chicago's major claims to culinary fame is the scrumptious deep-dish pizza with a chewy cornmeal crust that was developed by the founders of the renowned Pizzeria Uno in 1941. Like many Chicago pizzerias, you can make dough for deep-dish pizza without cornmeal; just use the California-Style Pizza Dough.

If necessary, review Making Perfect Pizza at Home (pages 9–25).

Make the Cornmeal Pizza Dough and set aside to rise as directed.

Prepare the Seasoned Tomato Pulp or Pizzeria-Style Tomato Sauce as directed and set aside to cool to room temperature.

Prepare an oven as directed for deep-dish pizza on page 21 and preheat it to 475 degrees F. Brush a 15-inch deep-dish pizza pan or two 9-inch pans with olive oil.

Place the ball of dough in the 15-inch pan, or divide the dough into 2 equal pieces and place each in a 9-inch pan. Starting in the middle, press the dough with your fingertips to cover the bottom and about 1 inch up the sides of the pan(s), making the dough thickness as even as possible. For a traditional crust, cover with plastic wrap or a cloth kitchen towel and let the dough rise in the pan(s) for about 20 minutes before filling. For a thinner crust, skip the rising.

Prick the bottom of the dough every ½ inch with a fork. Transfer the pan(s) to the bottom rack of the preheated oven and bake for 4 minutes.

Remove the pan(s) from the oven and lightly brush the crust(s) all over with olive oil. Quickly spread the mozzarella cheese completely over the bottom of the crust(s), dividing evenly if using 2 pans, then spoon on the tomato pulp or sauce. Sprinkle with the Parmesan cheese and top with the sausage. Drizzle with olive oil.

Return the pan(s) to the bottom rack of the oven and bake for 5 minutes, then move the pan(s) to a rack in the upper portion of the oven and bake until the crust is golden, the cheese is bubbly, and the sausage is cooked through, about 15 minutes longer.

Remove the pan(s) to a wire rack and let stand for about 5 minutes. If baked in a pan with a removable bottom, remove the pizza and transfer to a cutting tray or board. Lightly brush the edges of the crust(s) with olive oil. Sprinkle with the parsley. Slice and serve immediately.

Makes 8 servings

New York–Style Pizza

Neapolitan-Style Pizza Dough
(page 16)

1 cup Pizzeria-Style Tomato Sauce
(page 138)

Vegetable oil or cooking spray for
greasing pizza screen or
ventilated pizza pan (if using)

Cornmeal for sprinkling pizza peel
(if using)

Extra-virgin olive oil for brushing
crust and drizzling over
toppings

1½ teaspoons minced garlic

1½ tablespoons minced fresh
oregano, or 1½ teaspoons
crumbled dried oregano

3 cups freshly shredded high-quality
semisoft mozzarella cheese
(about 9 ounces), preferably
made with whole milk

Optional Toppings (choose one or a
combination):

6 to 8 flat anchovy fillets

1 cup cooked and crumbled sweet
Italian sausage

1 cup sautéed sliced fresh mushrooms

1 cup sliced pepperoni

1 cup sliced cooked Italian meatballs

1 cup sliced green or red sweet
pepper

1 cup peeled, seeded, well-drained,
and sliced ripe tomato

1 cup sliced red or yellow onion,
separated into rings

½ cup drained, pitted dry-cured black
olives, preferably from Italy

¼ cup freshly grated Parmesan
cheese (about 1 ounce), preferably Parmigiano-Reggiano

Freshly grated Parmesan cheese,
preferably Parmigiano-
Reggiano, for serving

Crushed dried chile for serving

Since America's first pizzeria, Lombardi's, was opened in New York in 1905 by a Neapolitan immigrant *pizzaiolo* ("pizza baker"), it's no surprise that New York–style pizza is similar to the traditional Neapolitan pie. The principal departure from its origin is the use of tomato sauce in place of fresh tomatoes, as full-flavored varieties were hard to come by on this side of the Atlantic in the early twentieth century. This pie became the standard of pizzerias coast to coast.

If necessary, review Making Perfect Pizza at Home (pages 9–25).

Make the Neapolitan-Style Pizza Dough and set aside to rise as directed.

Prepare the Pizzeria-Style Tomato Sauce as directed and set aside to cool to room temperature.

About 30 minutes before baking the pizza, prepare an oven as directed on page 21 and preheat it to 500 degrees F. If using a pizza screen or ventilated pan, brush it with vegetable oil or coat with spray and set aside. If baking directly on a stone or tiles, sprinkle a pizza peel with cornmeal and set aside.

On a lightly floured surface, roll out or stretch the dough and shape it as desired. Place the dough on the prepared screen, pan, or peel. Brush the dough all over with olive oil, then top with the tomato sauce, leaving a ½-inch border around the edges. Scatter the garlic and oregano over the sauce, then top with the mozzarella cheese. Arrange one or more of the toppings (if using) over the cheese. Sprinkle with the ¼ cup Parmesan cheese and drizzle with olive oil. If using a pizza peel, give it a quick, short jerk to be sure that the bottom of the crust has not stuck to it.

Transfer the pizza to the preheated oven and bake until the crust is golden, about 10 minutes.

Remove the pizza to a wire rack and let stand for about 2 minutes, then transfer to a cutting tray or board and lightly brush the edges of the crust with olive oil. Slice and serve immediately. Pass additional Parmesan cheese and crushed chile at the table for sprinkling over the pizza.

Makes 8 servings

Neapolitan-Style Pizza Dough (page 16) or California-Style Pizza Dough (page 18)

1 cup Pizzeria-Style Tomato Sauce (page 138)

Vegetable oil or cooking spray for greasing pizza screen or ventilated pizza pan (if using)

Cornmeal for sprinkling pizza peel (if using)

Extra-virgin olive oil for brushing crust and drizzling over toppings

7 ounces pepperoni, thinly sliced

3 cups freshly shredded high-quality semisoft mozzarella cheese (about 9 ounces), preferably made with whole milk

Freshly grated Parmesan cheese, preferably Parmigiano-Reggiano, for serving

Crushed dried chile for serving

Pepperoni Pizza

Pepperoni, a spicy beef and pork sausage that is air-dried and smoked, has long been America's favorite pizza topping. Like baseball, burgers, and hot dogs, our preferred pizza is uniquely American. In order to keep the edges of the pepperoni slices from curling up and drying out during baking, I put them underneath the cheese. If you prefer the traditional method and wish to see the slices atop the cheese, be sure to watch carefully near the end of baking to keep the pepperoni from burning.

If necessary, review Making Perfect Pizza at Home (pages 9–25).

Make the selected pizza dough and set aside to rise as directed.

Prepare the Pizzeria-Style Tomato Sauce as directed and set aside to cool to room temperature.

About 30 minutes before baking the pizza, prepare an oven as directed on page 21 and preheat it to 500 degrees F. If using a pizza screen or ventilated pan, brush it with vegetable oil or coat with spray and set aside. If baking directly on a stone or tiles, sprinkle a pizza peel with cornmeal and set aside.

On a lightly floured surface, roll out or stretch the dough and shape it as desired. Place the dough on the prepared screen, pan, or peel. Brush the dough all over with olive oil, then top with the tomato sauce, leaving a ½-inch border around the edges. Arrange the pepperoni in a single layer, overlapping the slices slightly. Distribute the mozzarella cheese over the pepperoni and drizzle evenly with olive oil. If using a pizza peel, give it a quick, short jerk to be sure that the bottom of the crust has not stuck to it.

Transfer the pizza to the preheated oven and bake until the crust is golden, about 10 minutes.

Remove the pizza to a wire rack and let stand for about 2 minutes, then transfer to a cutting tray or board and lightly brush the edges of the crust with olive oil. Slice and serve immediately. Pass Parmesan cheese and crushed chile for sprinkling over the pizza at the table.

Makes 8 servings

Red or White Clam Pizza

Whether you choose to make a white pie or a red tomato version, this long-popular New England pizza calls for the finest white Cheddar, not an orange-dyed type.

Neapolitan-Style Pizza Dough (page 16) or California-Style Pizza Dough (page 18)

Seasoned Tomato Pulp (page 136), or 1 cup Pizzeria-Style Tomato Sauce (page 138), if making a red pizza

Vegetable oil or cooking spray for greasing pizza screen or ventilated pizza pan (if using)

Cornmeal for sprinkling pizza peel (if using)

Extra-virgin olive oil for brushing crust and drizzling over toppings

2 tablespoons minced garlic, or to taste

3 cups freshly shredded white Cheddar cheese (about 9 ounces)

4 cups freshly shucked, chopped, and drained small clams, or 4 cans (10 ounces each) whole baby clams, drained

Salt

Freshly ground white pepper

½ cup freshly grated Parmesan cheese (about 2 ounces), preferably Parmigiano-Reggiano

2 tablespoons chopped fresh flat-leaf parsley

Crushed dried chile for serving

If necessary, review Making Perfect Pizza at Home (pages 9–25).

Make the selected pizza dough and set aside to rise as directed.

If making a red pizza, make the Seasoned Tomato Pulp or Pizzeria-Style Tomato Sauce as directed and set aside to cool to room temperature.

About 30 minutes before baking the pizza, prepare an oven as directed on page 21 and preheat it to 500 degrees F. If using a pizza screen or ventilated pan, brush it with vegetable oil or coat with spray and set aside. If baking directly on a stone or tiles, sprinkle a pizza peel with cornmeal and set aside.

On a lightly floured surface, roll out or stretch the dough and shape it as desired. Place the dough on the prepared screen, pan, or peel. Brush the dough all over with olive oil. If making a red pizza, spread with the tomato pulp or sauce. Sprinkle with the garlic and top with the Cheddar cheese, leaving a ½-inch border around the edges. Distribute the clams over the cheese, sprinkle with salt and pepper to taste, and drizzle with olive oil. If using a pizza peel, give it a quick, short jerk to be sure that the bottom of the crust has not stuck to it.

Transfer the pizza to the preheated oven and bake until the crust is golden, about 10 minutes.

Remove the pizza to a wire rack and let stand for about 2 minutes, then transfer to a cutting tray or board and lightly brush the edges of the crust with olive oil. Sprinkle with the Parmesan cheese and parsley. Slice and serve immediately. Offer crushed chile at the table.

Makes 8 servings

Two novel ways to serve pizza as appetizers open this chapter, followed by a varied assortment of nontraditional pizzas. A few are favorites of upscale American restaurants and others are my own innovations. Some die-hard detractors enjoy labeling such pies "designer" pizzas and proudly claim not to indulge in such non-Italian versions. Thankfully, most of us realize that even a tradition as wonderful as pizza can be expanded to embrace new ideas that result in pies that are as tasty as the classics.

50

Contempo-rary Pizzas

51

California-Style Pizza Dough (page
   18) or Herbed Pizza Dough
   (page 20)
Seasoned Tomato Pulp (page 136), or
   1 cup Pizzeria-Style Tomato
   Sauce (page 138)
Extra-virgin olive oil for brushing
1/2 cup freshly grated Parmesan
   cheese (about 2 ounces),
   preferably Parmigiano-
   Reggiano
1 tablespoon minced fresh oregano,
   or 1 teaspoon crumbled dried
   oregano

Pizza Sticks

Use pizza dough and a simple spread of tomato, cheese, and herbs to create sticks that are deli-cious appetizers or main-dish accompaniments. I often serve these alongside a big green salad for a perfect lunch. For a hearty appetizer, wrap thin slices of prosciutto around the pizza sticks.

Make the selected pizza dough and set aside to
rise as directed.

Make the Seasoned Tomato Pulp or Pizzeria-Style
Tomato Sauce as directed and set aside to cool to
room temperature.

Position racks so that the pizza sticks will bake in
the middle of an oven and preheat the oven to
425 degrees F. Line 2 baking sheets with kitchen
parchment and set aside.

On a lightly floured surface, roll out the dough
into a 12-inch square. Brush the dough all over
with oil, then spread with the tomato pulp or
sauce and sprinkle with the cheese and oregano.
Using a pizza cutter, slice the dough across one
side into 16 strips about 3/4 inch wide. Place the
strips about 2 inches apart on the prepared baking sheets. If desired, hold each strip at each end
and twist to form spirals.

Transfer the baking sheets to the preheated oven
and bake until the sticks are lightly golden, 10
to 12 minutes. If baking on 2 racks, rotate the baking sheets after about 5 minutes for more even
cooking.

Remove the sheets to a wire rack and let stand
for about 2 minutes, then lightly brush exposed
crusts with oil. Serve warm.

Makes 16 pizza sticks for 8 appetizer servings

California-Style Pizza Dough
(page 18)
3 cups freshly shredded high-quality
semisoft mozzarella cheese
(about 9 ounces), preferably
made with whole milk
¼ cup minced garlic
2 tablespoons extra-virgin olive oil
Vegetable oil or cooking spray for
greasing pizza screen or
ventilated pizza pan (if using)
Cornmeal for sprinkling pizza peel
(if using)
Extra-virgin olive oil for brushing
crust
1 cup freshly grated Parmesan
cheese (about 4 ounces),
preferably Parmigiano-
Reggiano

Pizza Chips

The idea for these appetizer pizza "chips" comes from Steamers, a lakeside café that specializes in pizza in Kings Beach, California. I've frequently enjoyed their garlicky version accompanied with a frosty margarita.

If necessary, review Making Perfect Pizza at Home (pages 9–25).

Make the California-Style Pizza Dough and set aside to rise as directed.

In a bowl, toss the mozzarella cheese with the garlic and the 2 tablespoons olive oil. Set aside.

About 30 minutes before baking the pizza, prepare an oven as directed on page 21 and preheat it to 500 degrees F. If using a pizza screen or ventilated pan, brush it with vegetable oil or coat with spray and set aside. If baking directly on a stone or tiles, sprinkle a pizza peel with cornmeal and set aside.

On a lightly floured surface, roll out or stretch the dough as thinly as possible and shape it into 1 large round. Place the dough on the prepared screen, pan, or peel. Brush the dough all over with olive oil, then top with the mozzarella-garlic mixture, leaving a ½-inch border around the edges. Sprinkle with ½ cup of the Parmesan cheese. If using a pizza peel, give it a quick, short jerk to be sure that the bottom of the crust has not stuck to it.

Transfer the pizza to the preheated oven and bake until the crust is golden, about 10 minutes.

Remove the pizza to a wire rack and let stand for about 2 minutes, then transfer to a cutting tray or

board and lightly brush the edges of the crust with olive oil. Sprinkle with the remaining ½ cup Parmesan cheese. Slice into numerous pieces about the size of corn tortilla chips and serve immediately.

Makes 8 servings

Variation
Top the mozzarella-garlic mixture with minced fresh hot chiles or crushed dried chile and/or Seasoned Tomato Pulp (page 136) to taste before sprinkling on the Parmesan.

California-Style Pizza Dough
    (page 18)
1 large garlic head
Vegetable oil or cooking spray for
    greasing pizza screen or
    ventilated pizza pan (if using)
Cornmeal for sprinkling pizza peel
    (if using)
2 cups freshly shredded high-quality
    semisoft mozzarella cheese
    (about 6 ounces), preferably
    made with whole milk
1 cup crumbled fresh or semidry mild
    goat cheese (about 4 ounces)
Extra-virgin olive oil for brushing
    crust and drizzling over
    toppings
½ cup slivered, drained sun-dried
    tomatoes packed in olive oil
Salt
Freshly ground black pepper
¼ cup freshly grated Parmesan
    cheese (about 1 ounce),
    preferably Parmigiano-
    Reggiano

California Classic Pizza

This is the topping combination that began the new wave of pizza baking in America. I've dubbed this pie California Classic because it calls for the Golden State's culinary "holy trinity": goat cheese, roasted garlic, and sun-dried tomatoes.

If necessary, review Making Perfect Pizza at Home (pages 9–25).

Make the California-Style Pizza Dough and set aside to rise as directed.

Prepare an oven as directed on page 21, position a rack in the middle of the oven for roasting the garlic, and preheat the oven to 350 degrees F.

Roast the garlic in the preheated oven as directed on page 139 and set aside to cool completely.

About 30 minutes before baking the pizza, pre-heat the oven to 500 degrees F. If using a pizza screen or ventilated pan, brush it with vegetable oil or coat with spray and set aside. If baking directly on a stone or tiles, sprinkle a pizza peel with cornmeal and set aside.

In a bowl, combine the mozzarella and goat cheeses and set aside.

On a lightly floured surface, roll out or stretch the dough and shape it as desired. Place the dough on the prepared screen, pan, or peel. Brush the dough all over with olive oil. Squeeze the roasted garlic from the skin onto the dough and smear with a dull knife or small metal spatula to spread evenly, leaving a ½-inch border around the edges. Top with the cheese mixture, then scatter the tomatoes over the cheese. Season to taste with salt and pepper and drizzle with olive oil. If

using a pizza peel, give it a quick, short jerk to be sure that the bottom of the crust has not stuck to it.

Transfer the pizza to the preheated oven and bake until the crust is golden, about 10 minutes.

Remove the pizza to a wire rack and let stand for about 2 minutes, then transfer to a cutting tray or board and lightly brush the edges of the crust with olive oil. Sprinkle with the Parmesan cheese. Slice and serve immediately.

Makes 8 servings

California-Style Pizza Dough (page 18) or Neapolitan-Style Pizza Dough (page 16)

3 large red sweet peppers

Vegetable oil or cooking spray for greasing pizza screen or ventilated pizza pan (if using)

Cornmeal for sprinkling pizza peel (if using)

Extra-virgin olive oil for brushing crust and drizzling over toppings

3 cups freshly shredded high-quality semisoft mozzarella cheese (about 9 ounces), preferably made with whole milk

5 or 6 flat anchovy fillets, minced

2 teaspoons minced garlic

2 1/2 cups chopped, pitted dry-cured black olives, preferably from Italy

Salt

Freshly ground black pepper

Black Olive and Roasted Red Pepper Pizza

I like to form a square crust and arrange the red and black toppings in a checkerboard design. For this preparation, I prefer wrinkled black olives from Italy that have been dry-cured and coated in olive oil, although any favorite Mediterranean-style olives can be substituted.

If necessary, review Making Perfect Pizza at Home (pages 9–25).

Make the selected pizza dough and set aside to rise as directed.

Roast the sweet peppers as directed on page 139. Chop finely and set aside.

About 30 minutes before baking the pizza, prepare an oven as directed on page 21 and preheat it to 500 degrees F. If using a pizza screen or ventilated pan, brush it with vegetable oil or coat with spray and set aside. If baking directly on a stone or tiles, sprinkle a pizza peel with cornmeal and set aside.

On a lightly floured surface, roll out or stretch the dough and shape it as desired. Place the dough on the prepared screen, pan, or peel. Brush the dough all over with olive oil, then top with the mozzarella cheese, leaving a 1/2-inch border around the edges. Sprinkle with the anchovies and garlic, then arrange the reserved red pepper and the olives in alternating stripes or in a checkerboard design. Season to taste with salt and pepper and drizzle with olive oil. If using a pizza peel, give it a quick, short jerk to be sure that the bottom of the crust has not stuck to it.

Transfer the pizza to the preheated oven and bake until the crust is golden, about 10 minutes.

Remove the pizza to a wire rack and let stand for about 2 minutes, then transfer to a cutting tray or board and lightly brush the edges of the crust with olive oil. Slice and serve immediately.

Makes 8 servings

California-Style Pizza Dough (page 18) or Neapolitan-Style Pizza Dough (page 16)

Pesto

2 cups firmly packed fresh basil leaves

¼ cup pine nuts

1 teaspoon minced garlic

1 teaspoon red wine vinegar or balsamic vinegar (optional)

½ cup extra-virgin olive oil

¾ cup freshly grated Parmesan cheese (about 3 ounces), preferably Parmigiano-Reggiano, or a mixture of ½ cup Parmesan and ¼ cup pecorino romano cheeses

Salt

Vegetable oil or cooking spray for greasing pizza screen or ventilated pizza pan (if using)

Cornmeal for sprinkling pizza peel (if using)

1½ cups freshly shredded high-quality semisoft mozzarella cheese (about 4½ ounces), preferably made with whole milk

1½ cups freshly shredded Italian Fontina cheese (about 7½ ounces)

Extra-virgin olive oil for brushing crust and drizzling over toppings

¼ cup freshly grated Parmesan cheese (about 1 ounce), preferably Parmigiano-Reggiano

Tiny whole fresh basil leaves for garnish

Pine nuts for garnish

Pesto Pizza

Even though today "pesto" is being made from cilantro, mint, parsley, spinach, or almost anything green, I remain partial to the traditional recipe using fresh basil. The sauce can be made up to several days ahead and stored in the refrigerator with a thin layer of olive oil covering the top to prevent darkening. Since cooking destroys the delicate flavor of basil, I always top the pizza with the sauce after it comes out of the oven.

If necessary, review Making Perfect Pizza at Home (pages 9–25).

Make the selected pizza dough and set aside to rise as directed.

To make the Pesto, in a food processor, combine the basil, pine nuts, garlic, and vinegar (if using) and chop finely. With the machine running, slowly add the oil, continuing to blend until well mixed. Transfer to a bowl, stir in the cheese, and season to taste with salt. Alternatively (and traditionally), grind the basil, pine nuts, and garlic in a mortar with a pestle before working in the remaining ingredients. Set aside.

About 30 minutes before baking the pizza, prepare an oven as directed on page 21 and preheat it to 500 degrees F. If using a pizza screen or ventilated pan, brush it with vegetable oil or coat with spray and set aside. If baking directly on a stone or tiles, sprinkle a pizza peel with cornmeal and set aside.

In a bowl, combine the mozzarella and Fontina cheeses and set aside.

On a lightly floured surface, roll out or stretch the dough and shape it as desired. Place the dough on the prepared screen, pan, or peel. Prick the dough all over with a fork and brush it with olive oil, then top with the cheese mixture, leaving a ½-inch border around the edges. Drizzle with olive oil. If using a pizza peel, give it a quick, short jerk to be sure that the bottom of the crust has not stuck to it.

Transfer the pizza to the preheated oven and bake until the crust is golden, about 10 minutes.

Remove the pizza to a wire rack and let stand for about 2 minutes, then transfer to a cutting tray or board and lightly brush the edges of the crust with olive oil. Spoon on the Pesto to taste, sprinkle with the Parmesan cheese, and garnish with basil leaves and pine nuts. Slice and serve immediately.

Makes 8 servings

Variation

For Chicken Pesto Pizza, distribute about 2 cups shredded cooked chicken over the cheese before baking.

California-Style Pizza Dough (page 18) or Neapolitan-Style Pizza Dough (page 16)

Vegetable oil or cooking spray for greasing pizza screen or ventilated pizza pan (if using)

Cornmeal for sprinkling pizza peel (if using)

Extra-virgin olive oil for brushing crust and drizzling over toppings

3 cups crumbled fresh mild goat cheese (about 12 ounces)

2 jars (6½ ounces each) high-quality marinated artichoke hearts, well drained and thinly sliced

½ cup chopped walnuts (optional)

¼ cup freshly grated Parmesan cheese (about 1 ounce), preferably Parmigiano-Reggiano

2 tablespoons chopped fresh chervil or flat-leaf parsley

Artichoke and Goat Cheese Pizza

This recipe was created at the request of Mary Whitney. My partner, Andrew, gives lessons to Mary in his downstairs music studio, and her beautiful operatic soprano voice often wafts through my kitchen when I'm cooking. My dishes always seem to taste better when made to such glorious musical accompaniment.

If necessary, review Making Perfect Pizza at Home (pages 9–26).

Make the selected pizza dough and set aside to rise as directed.

About 30 minutes before baking the pizza, prepare an oven as directed on page 21 and preheat it to 500 degrees F. If using a pizza screen or ventilated pan, brush it with vegetable oil or coat with spray and set aside. If baking directly on a stone or tiles, sprinkle a pizza peel with cornmeal and set aside.

On a lightly floured surface, roll out or stretch the dough and shape it as desired. Place the dough on the prepared screen, pan, or peel. Brush the dough all over with olive oil, then top with the goat cheese, leaving a ½-inch border around the edges. Distribute the artichoke slices and walnuts (if using) over the cheese and drizzle with olive oil. If using a pizza peel, give it a quick, short jerk to be sure that the bottom of the crust has not stuck to it.

Transfer the pizza to the preheated oven and bake until the crust is golden, about 10 minutes.

Remove the pizza to a wire rack and let stand for about 2 minutes, then transfer to a cutting tray or

board and lightly brush the edges of the crust with olive oil. Sprinkle with the Parmesan cheese and chervil or parsley. Slice and serve immediately.

Makes 8 servings

Neapolitan-Style Pizza Dough (page 16) or California-Style Pizza Dough (page 18)

2 pounds summer squash such as crookneck, pattypan, or zucchini, one type or a combination

Salt

Extra-virgin olive oil for brushing squash and crust and drizzling over toppings

Vegetable oil or cooking spray for greasing pizza screen or ventilated pizza pan (if using)

Cornmeal for sprinkling pizza peel (if using)

2 tablespoons coarsely chopped garlic

3 cups crumbled feta or fresh mild goat cheese (about 12 ounces)

1/4 cup minced fresh herbs such as summer savory, marjoram, and thyme, one type or a combination

2 tablespoons grated or minced fresh lemon zest, or more to taste

Herbed Summer Squash Pizza

During the peak of the summer squash harvest, try this intriguing combination of young, tender squash and tangy feta or goat cheese showered with fresh herbs. A scattering of fresh lemon zest adds a piquant accent to the pie.

If necessary, review Making Perfect Pizza at Home (pages 9–25).

Make the selected pizza dough and set aside to rise as directed.

Cut the squash crosswise into slices about 1/4 inch thick. Sprinkle both sides of each slice with salt and place in a colander. Set the colander over a bowl or in a sink and let stand for about 30 minutes to draw out excess moisture.

Meanwhile, prepare an oven as directed on page 21, position a rack in the middle of the oven for roasting the squash, and preheat the oven to 350 degrees F.

Gather the squash in your hands and squeeze gently to release as much liquid as possible, then pat dry with paper toweling. (First rinse the slices under cold running water if you wish to rid them of excess salt.) Brush the squash slices on both sides with olive oil and place in a single layer on a baking sheet. Transfer to the preheated oven and roast the squash until tender, about 20 minutes.

Remove the baking sheet from the oven and set aside to cool the squash to room temperature.

About 30 minutes before baking the pizza, preheat the oven to 500 degrees F. If using a pizza screen or ventilated pan, brush it with vegetable oil or coat with spray and set aside. If baking directly on a stone or tiles, sprinkle a pizza peel with cornmeal and set aside.

On a lightly floured surface, roll out or stretch the dough and shape it as desired. Place the dough on the prepared screen, pan, or peel. Brush the dough all over with olive oil, then sprinkle with the garlic and top with the cheese, leaving a 1/2-inch border around the edges. Distribute the squash slices over the cheese, sprinkle with 2 tablespoons of the minced herbs, and drizzle with olive oil. If using a pizza peel, give it a quick, short jerk to be sure that the bottom of the crust has not stuck to it.

Transfer the pizza to the preheated oven and bake until the crust is golden, about 10 minutes.

Remove the pizza to a wire rack and let stand for about 2 minutes, then transfer to a cutting tray or board and lightly brush the edges of the crust with olive oil. Sprinkle with the remaining 2 tablespoons minced herbs and the lemon zest. Slice and serve immediately.

Makes 8 servings

California-Style Pizza Dough (page
    18) or Herbed Pizza Dough
    (page 20)
2 tablespoons extra-virgin olive oil
1 cup sliced leek, including pale
    green portion
1/2 cup sliced green onion, including
    green tops
1/2 cup sliced green garlic, or
    1 tablespoon minced garlic
Salt
Freshly ground black pepper
Vegetable oil or cooking spray for
    greasing pizza screen or
    ventilated pizza pan (if using)
Cornmeal for sprinkling pizza peel
    (if using)
Extra-virgin olive oil for brushing
    crust and drizzling over
    toppings
2 cups freshly shredded high-quality
    semisoft mozzarella cheese
    (about 6 ounces), preferably
    made with whole milk
1 cup crumbled fresh mild goat
    cheese (about 4 ounces)
1/2 teaspoon crushed dried chile, or
    to taste
2 tablespoons chopped fresh chives
    or garlic chives

Spring Onion Pizza

In the spring, farmers' markets and specialty produce stores feature small tender leeks and green garlic, tender shoots of garlic that form before the bulb end divides into separate cloves. Teamed with their common green onion relatives, they make a fresh and delicate topping for pizza.

If necessary, review Making Perfect Pizza at Home (pages 9–25).

Make the selected pizza dough and set aside to rise as directed.

In a sauté pan or skillet, heat the 2 tablespoons olive oil over medium-high heat. Add the leek, green onion, and green garlic or garlic and cook, stirring frequently, until soft, about 5 minutes. Season to taste with salt and pepper. Set aside to cool to room temperature.

About 30 minutes before baking the pizza, prepare an oven as directed on page 21 and preheat it to 500 degrees F. If using a pizza screen or ventilated pan, brush it with vegetable oil or coat with spray and set aside. If baking directly on a stone or tiles, sprinkle a pizza peel with cornmeal and set aside.

On a lightly floured surface, roll out or stretch the dough and shape it as desired. Place the dough on the prepared screen, pan, or peel. Brush the dough all over with olive oil, then top with the mozzarella, leaving a 1/2-inch border around the edges. Distribute the leek mixture over the cheese, sprinkle with the goat cheese and the crushed chile, and drizzle with olive oil. If using a pizza peel, give it a quick, short jerk to be sure that the bottom of the crust has not stuck to it.

Transfer the pizza to the preheated oven and bake until the crust is golden, about 10 minutes.

Remove the pizza to a wire rack and let stand for about 2 minutes, then transfer to a cutting tray or board and lightly brush the edges of the crust with olive oil. Sprinkle with the chives. Slice and serve immediately.

Makes 8 servings

California-Style Pizza Dough
(page 18)
2 pounds small globe eggplants
Salt
Extra-virgin olive oil for brushing
eggplant and crust and drizzling
over toppings
Vegetable oil or cooking spray for
greasing pizza screen or
ventilated pizza pan (if using)
Cornmeal for sprinkling pizza peel
(if using)
1 cup freshly shredded high-quality
semisoft mozzarella cheese
(about 3 ounces), preferably
made with whole milk
1 cup crumbled fresh mild goat
cheese (about 4 ounces)
1 cup freshly grated Parmesan
cheese, preferably Parmigiano-
Reggiano, or pecorino romano
cheese (about 4 ounces)
2 teaspoons minced garlic
1 tablespoon minced mixed fresh
aromatic herbs such as marjoram, rosemary, and thyme;
or 1 teaspoon crumbled dried
herbes de Provence, or to taste
Freshly ground black pepper

Eggplant Pizza

This pairing of tender eggplant and a trio of cheeses is a perfect marriage of flavors. If desired, spoon Seasoned Tomato Pulp (page 136) over the cheeses before adding the eggplant.

If necessary, review Making Perfect Pizza at Home (pages 9–25).

Make the California-Style Pizza Dough and set aside to rise as directed.

Cut the eggplants crosswise into 1/4-inch-thick slices. Sprinkle both sides of each eggplant slice with salt. Lay the slices on paper toweling, cover with more paper toweling, top with a cutting board and heavy weights (such as canned foods), and let stand for about 30 minutes to draw out excess moisture.

Meanwhile, prepare an oven as directed on page 21, position a rack in the middle of the oven for roasting the eggplant, and preheat the oven to 400 degrees F.

Using paper toweling, blot off as much salt and moisture as possible from the eggplant slices. (First rinse the slices under cold running water if you wish to rid them of the excess salt.) Brush the slices on both sides with olive oil and place in a single layer on a baking sheet. Transfer to the preheated oven and roast the eggplant slices until lightly browned and tender, about 15 minutes.

Remove the baking sheet from the oven and set aside to cool the eggplant to room temperature.

About 30 minutes before baking the pizza, pre-heat the oven to 500 degrees F. If using a pizza screen or ventilated pan, brush it with vegetable oil or coat with spray and set aside. If baking directly on a stone or tiles, sprinkle a pizza peel with cornmeal and set aside.

In a bowl, combine the mozzarella, goat, and Parmesan cheeses and set aside.

On a lightly floured surface, roll out or stretch the dough and shape it as desired. Place the dough on the prepared screen, pan, or peel. Brush the dough all over with olive oil, then cover with the cheese mixture, leaving a 1/2-inch border around the edges. Sprinkle with the garlic and 1 1/2 tea-spoons of the fresh herbs or the 1 teaspoon dried herbs. Top with the eggplant slices and drizzle evenly with olive oil. Sprinkle with pepper to taste. If using a pizza peel, give it a quick, short jerk to be sure that the bottom of the crust has not stuck to it.

Transfer the pizza to the preheated oven and bake until the crust is golden, about 10 minutes.

Remove the pizza to a wire rack and let stand for about 2 minutes, then transfer to a cutting tray or board and lightly brush the edges of the crust with olive oil. Sprinkle with the remaining 1 1/2 teaspoons fresh herbs (if using). Slice and serve immediately.

Makes 8 servings

Cornmeal Pizza Dough (page 20)

Vegetable oil or cooking spray for
greasing pizza screen or
ventilated pizza pan (if using)

Cornmeal for dusting pizza peel
(if using)

Extra-virgin olive oil for brushing
crust and drizzling over
toppings

3 cups freshly shredded hot-pepper
Monterey Jack cheese (about
9 ounces)

2 cups well-drained, cooked dried or
canned pinto beans

3 tablespoons sliced fresh or pickled
jalapeño chile, or to taste

¼ cup chopped fresh cilantro
(coriander)

Condiments

Fresh Tomato Salsa (a favorite recipe
or high-quality commercial
product)

Guacamole (a favorite recipe)

Mexican cultured cream (crema) or
sour cream

A cornmeal crust approximates the corn tortilla chips used in making nachos, a perennial Tex-Mex favorite. Offer the condiments at the table for diners to spoon atop each slice as desired. Mexican beers or frosty margaritas are the perfect beverages for this zesty pie.

If necessary, review Making Perfect Pizza at Home (pages 9–25).

Make the Cornmeal Pizza Dough and set aside to rise as directed.

About 30 minutes before baking the pizza, prepare an oven as directed on page 21 and preheat it to 500 degrees F. If using a pizza screen or ventilated pan, brush it with vegetable oil or coat with spray and set aside. If baking directly on a stone or tiles, sprinkle a pizza peel with cornmeal and set aside.

On a lightly floured surface, roll out or stretch the dough and shape it as desired. Place the dough on the prepared screen, pan, or peel. Brush the dough all over with olive oil, then top with the cheese, leaving a ½-inch border around the edges. Scatter the beans and chile over the cheese and drizzle evenly with olive oil. If using a pizza peel, give it a quick, short jerk to be sure that the bottom of the crust has not stuck to it.

Transfer the pizza to the preheated oven and bake until the crust is golden, about 10 minutes.

Remove the pizza to a wire rack and let stand for about 2 minutes, then transfer to a cutting tray or board and lightly brush the edges of the crust with olive oil. Sprinkle with the cilantro. Slice and serve immediately. Pass the condiments at the table for adding to the pizza.

Makes 8 servings

Cornmeal Pizza Dough (page 20)

8 medium-sized ears corn, shucked

2 tablespoons unsalted butter

2 teaspoons minced garlic, or
to taste

Salt

Freshly ground white pepper

Vegetable oil or cooking spray for
greasing pizza screen or
ventilated pizza pan (if using)

Cornmeal for sprinkling pizza peel
(if using)

2 cups freshly shredded high-quality
semisoft mozzarella cheese
(about 6 ounces), preferably
made with whole milk

1 cup freshly shredded smoked
Gouda, mozzarella, or other
smoked cheese (about 4
ounces)

Extra-virgin olive oil for brushing
crust and drizzling over
toppings

½ cup slivered, drained sun-dried
tomatoes packed in olive oil
(optional)

⅓ cup finely chopped red onion

½ cup freshly grated Parmesan
cheese (about 2 ounces),
preferably Parmigiano-
Reggiano

¼ cup minced fresh herb such as
chives, sage, or summer
savory

Corn Pizza

Inspired by a pizza that I enjoyed many years ago at Pizzeria Viccolo in San Francisco, I created this summer treat for my *Corn Cookbook,* now sadly out of print. When I've had my fill of corn on the cob, this delectable concoction renews my enthusiasm for sweet fresh corn. And teaming it with a cornmeal crust heightens the corn flavor.

If necessary, review Making Perfect Pizza at Home (pages 9–25).

Make the Cornmeal Pizza Dough and set aside to rise as directed.

Rest the base of an ear of corn on a large, deep plate or inside a large bowl. With a sharp knife, cut down the length of the cob from the tip to the base. Leave behind a bit of pulp to avoid mixing tough corn fibers into the corn. Rotate the ear until you have stripped it of kernels. Turn the knife blade over and scrape the cob with the blunt edge to remove the pulp and milky juices. Repeat with the remaining ears of corn. There should be about 4 cups kernels.

In a sauté pan or skillet, melt the butter over medium heat. Add the corn and garlic and cook, stirring frequently, until the corn is tender, about 4 minutes for young corn or for up to 8 minutes for older corn. Season to taste with salt and pepper. Transfer to a bowl and set aside to cool to room temperature.

About 30 minutes before baking the pizza, prepare an oven as directed on page 21 and preheat it to 500 degrees F. If using a pizza screen or ventilated pan, brush it with vegetable oil or coat with spray and set aside. If baking directly on a stone or tiles, sprinkle a pizza peel with cornmeal and set aside.

In a bowl, combine the mozzarella and smoked cheeses and set aside.

On a lightly floured surface, roll out or stretch the dough and shape it as desired. Place the dough on the prepared screen, pan, or peel. Brush the dough all over with olive oil, then top with the cheese mixture, leaving a ½-inch border around the edges. Scatter the tomatoes over the cheese, then top with the corn, sprinkle with the onion, and drizzle with olive oil. If using a pizza peel, give it a quick, short jerk to be sure that the bottom of the crust has not stuck to it.

Transfer the pizza to the preheated oven and bake until the crust is golden, about 10 minutes.

Remove the pizza to a wire rack and let stand for about 2 minutes, then transfer to a cutting tray or board and lightly brush the edges of the crust with olive oil. Sprinkle with the Parmesan cheese and herb of choice. Slice and serve immediately.

Makes 8 servings

California-Style Pizza Dough
(page 18)

Seasoned Tomato Pulp (page 136)

2 tablespoons minced canned
chipotle chiles packed in
adobo sauce, or more to taste

2 tablespoons adobo sauce
from canned chipotle chiles,
or more to taste

6 to 8 fresh medium-hot chiles such
as New Mexico or poblano

Vegetable oil or cooking spray for
greasing pizza screen or
ventilated pizza pan (if using)

Cornmeal for sprinkling pizza peel
(if using)

2 cups freshly shredded white
Cheddar cheese (about 6
ounces)

1 cup freshly shredded smoked
Gouda or other smoked cheese
(about 4 ounces)

Extra-virgin olive oil for brushing
crust and drizzling over
toppings

¼ cup fresh cilantro (coriander)
leaves

Fire and Smoke Pizza

Fiery roasted chiles team with smoky cheese to create this seductive pizza. And more fire and smoke come with the addition of chipotle chiles, which are smoked dried jalapeños.

If necessary, review Making Perfect Pizza at Home (pages 9–25).

Make the California-Style Pizza Dough and set aside to rise as directed.

Prepare the Seasoned Tomato Pulp as directed. Stir in the minced chipotle chiles and adobo sauce. Set aside to cool to room temperature.

Roast the fresh chiles as directed on page 139. Cut into narrow strips and set aside.

About 30 minutes before baking the pizza, prepare an oven as directed on page 21 and preheat it to 500 degrees F. If using a pizza screen or ventilated pan, brush it with vegetable oil or coat with spray and set aside. If baking directly on a stone or tiles, sprinkle a pizza peel with cornmeal and set aside.

In a bowl, combine the Cheddar and smoked cheeses and set aside.

On a lightly floured surface, roll out or stretch the dough and shape it as desired. Place the dough on the prepared screen, pan, or peel. Brush the dough all over with olive oil, then spread with the tomato-chipotle mixture, leaving a ½-inch border around the edges. Top with the cheese mixture, then arrange the roasted chile strips over the cheese and drizzle evenly with olive oil. If using a pizza peel, give it a quick, short jerk to

be sure that the bottom of the crust has not stuck to it.

Transfer the pizza to the preheated oven and bake until the crust is golden, about 10 minutes.

Remove the pizza to a wire rack and let stand for about 2 minutes, then transfer to a cutting tray or board and lightly brush the edges of the crust with olive oil. Sprinkle with the cilantro. Slice and serve immediately.

Makes 8 servings

California-Style Pizza Dough (page 18) or Neapolitan-Style Pizza Dough (page 16)

Tapénade

½ cup drained, pitted brine-cured Mediterranean-style ripe olives

¼ cup firmly packed fresh basil leaves

1½ tablespoons drained small capers

1 tablespoon coarsely chopped garlic

1 flat anchovy fillet

1 teaspoon finely grated or minced fresh lemon zest

2 tablespoons extra-virgin olive oil

1 tablespoon freshly squeezed lemon juice, or more if needed

Freshly ground black pepper

1 pound small flavorful boiling potatoes such as Yukon Gold

1 tablespoon extra-virgin olive oil

Salt

Freshly ground black pepper

Vegetable oil or cooking spray for greasing pizza screen or ventilated pizza pan (if using)

Cornmeal for sprinkling pizza peel (if using)

Extra-virgin olive oil for brushing crust and drizzling over toppings

2 cups freshly shredded high-quality semisoft mozzarella cheese (about 6 ounces), preferably made with whole milk

1 cup crumbled Stilton or other blue cheese (about 4 ounces)

1 cup fresh watercress leaves or pepper cress sprigs

Roasted Potato and Tapénade Pizza

Tapénade, the piquant olive paste from Provence, has become a staple of the contemporary American kitchen. Traditionally used as a spread for bread or accent for grilled fare, it makes a wonderful topping for pizza. To make a vegetarian pizza, omit the anchovy fillets from the tapénade and season the mixture with salt to taste.

If necessary, review Making Perfect Pizza at Home (pages 9–25).

Make the selected pizza dough and set aside to rise as directed.

To make the Tapénade, in a food processor, combine the olives, basil, capers, garlic, anchovy fillet, lemon zest, and olive oil. Puree until fairly smooth. Season to taste with lemon juice and pepper and blend well. Transfer to a bowl and set aside.

Prepare an oven as directed on page 21, position a rack in the middle of the oven for roasting the potatoes, and preheat the oven to 400 degrees F.

Slice the potatoes about ⅛ inch thick. In a bowl, toss them with the 1 tablespoon olive oil. Arrange the slices on a baking sheet in a single layer and sprinkle with salt and pepper to taste. Transfer to the preheated oven and roast the potatoes until they are tender when pierced with a wooden skewer or small, sharp knife but are not browned, about 15 minutes. Using a spatula, transfer the potato slices to a plate and set aside to cool to room temperature.

About 30 minutes before baking the pizza, preheat the oven to 500 degrees F. If using a pizza screen or ventilated pan, brush it with vegetable oil or coat with spray and set aside. If baking directly on a stone or tiles, sprinkle a pizza peel with cornmeal and set aside.

On a lightly floured surface, roll out or stretch the dough and shape it as desired. Place the dough on the prepared screen, pan, or peel. Brush the dough all over with olive oil, then top with the mozzarella, leaving a ½-inch border around the edges. Spoon small dollops of the Tapénade as evenly as possible over the cheese. Arrange the potato slices on top, then sprinkle with the blue cheese and drizzle with olive oil. If using a pizza peel, give it a quick, short jerk to be sure that the bottom of the crust has not stuck to it.

Transfer the pizza to the preheated oven and bake until the crust is golden, about 10 minutes.

Remove the pizza to a wire rack and let stand for about 2 minutes, then transfer to a cutting tray or board and lightly brush the edges of the crust with olive oil. Sprinkle with the watercress or pepper cress. Slice and serve immediately.

Makes 8 servings

California-Style Pizza Dough (page 18) or Neapolitan-Style Pizza Dough (page 16)

3 tablespoons olive oil

8 ounces thickly sliced pancetta (Italian unsmoked bacon), cut into small pieces

3 cups chopped leek, including pale green portion

Vegetable oil or cooking spray for greasing pizza screen or ventilated pizza pan (if using)

Cornmeal for sprinkling pizza peel (if using)

Extra-virgin olive oil for brushing crust and drizzling over toppings

2 cups freshly shredded Italian Fontina cheese (about 10 ounces)

About 20 fresh figs, halved length-wise

1/4 cup freshly grated Parmesan cheese (about 1 ounce), preferably Parmigiano-Reggiano

Leek, Fig, Pancetta, and Fontina Pizza

In this exotic pie, sweet leeks and figs provide a counterpoint to the salty and peppery Italian bacon that crowns the rich sea of cheese. The nutty flavor and satiny texture of Fontina make it one of my favorite Italian imports.

If necessary, review Making Perfect Pizza at Home (pages 9–25).

Make the selected pizza dough and set aside to rise as directed.

In a large sauté pan or heavy skillet, heat the 3 tablespoons olive oil over medium heat. Add the pancetta and cook, stirring frequently, until the meat is translucent, about 5 minutes. Using a slotted utensil, remove the pancetta to a bowl and set aside.

Add the leek to the pan in which the pancetta was cooked, and cook, stirring frequently, until tender but not browned, about 8 minutes. Remove from the heat and add to the pancetta. Set the mixture aside to cool to room temperature.

About 30 minutes before baking the pizza, pre-pare an oven as directed on page 21 and preheat it to 500 degrees F. If using a pizza screen or ven-tilated pan, brush it with vegetable oil or coat with spray and set aside. If baking directly on a stone or tiles, sprinkle a pizza peel with cornmeal and set aside.

On a lightly floured surface, roll out or stretch the dough and shape it as desired. Place the dough on the prepared screen, pan, or peel. Brush the dough all over with olive oil, then cover with the

Fontina cheese, leaving a 1/2-inch border around the edges. Distribute the pancetta-leek mixture over the cheese, then arrange the figs, cut sides up, on top and drizzle them evenly with olive oil. If using a pizza peel, give it a quick, short jerk to be sure that the bottom of the crust has not stuck to it.

Transfer the pizza to the preheated oven and bake until the crust is golden, about 10 minutes.

Remove the pizza to a wire rack and let stand for about 2 minutes, then transfer to a cutting tray or board and lightly brush the edges of the crust with olive oil. Sprinkle with the Parmesan cheese. Slice and serve immediately.

Makes 8 servings

California-Style Pizza Dough (page 18) or Neapolitan-Style Pizza Dough (page 16)

2 large garlic heads

Vegetable oil or cooking spray for greasing pizza screen or ventilated pizza pan (if using)

Cornmeal for sprinkling pizza peel (if using)

1/2 cup pitted dried sour cherries

Brandy or Cognac for soaking cherries

1 1/2 cups freshly shredded high-quality semisoft mozzarella cheese (about 4 1/2 ounces), preferably made with whole milk

1 1/2 cups crumbled Gorgonzola cheese (about 6 ounces)

Extra-virgin olive oil for brushing crust and drizzling over toppings

6 ounces thickly sliced prosciutto, cut into slivers

2 cups mâche, mizuna, tatsoi, or other small, tender greens

1 tablespoon extra-virgin olive oil

1 teaspoon freshly squeezed lemon juice

Salt

Freshly ground black pepper

Roasted Garlic and Gorgonzola Pizza

Aged Gorgonzola may overpower the other ingredients, so when creamy fresh Gorgonzola is not available, choose another favorite blue cheese as a substitute for this luxurious Italian import. A glass of hearty red wine matches the robust flavors of this pie.

If necessary, review Making Perfect Pizza at Home (pages 9–25).

Make the selected pizza dough and set aside to rise as directed.

Prepare an oven as directed on page 21, position a rack in the middle of the oven for roasting the garlic, and preheat the oven to 350 degrees F.

Roast the garlic as directed on page 139. Set aside to cool slightly, then squeeze the garlic from the skins onto a cutting surface. Using a small, sharp knife, chop the garlic coarsely and set it aside.

About 30 minutes before baking the pizza, pre-heat the oven to 500 degrees F. If using a pizza screen or ventilated pan, brush it with vegetable oil or coat with spray and set aside. If baking directly on a stone or tiles, sprinkle a pizza peel with cornmeal and set aside.

In a small bowl, combine the cherries with enough brandy or Cognac to cover barely and set aside until the cherries are soft and plumped, about 15 minutes.

In a bowl, combine the mozzarella and Gorgon-zola cheeses and set aside.

On a lightly floured surface, roll out or stretch the dough and shape it as desired. Place the dough on the prepared screen, pan, or peel. Brush the dough all over with olive oil, then sprinkle with the roasted garlic, leaving a 1/2-inch border around the edges. Top with the cheese mixture. Drain the soaked cherries well and sprinkle them and the prosciutto over the cheese, then drizzle with olive oil. If using a pizza peel, give it a quick, short jerk to be sure that the bottom of the crust has not stuck to it.

Transfer the pizza to the preheated oven and bake until the crust is golden, about 10 minutes.

Remove the pizza to a wire rack and let stand for about 2 minutes.

Meanwhile, in a bowl, toss the greens with the 1 tablespoon olive oil, the lemon juice, and salt and pepper to taste.

Transfer the pizza to a cutting tray or board and lightly brush the edges of the crust with olive oil. Sprinkle with the greens. Slice and serve immedi-ately.

Makes 8 servings

Wild Mushroom Pizza

California-Style Pizza Dough (page 18) or Neapolitan-Style Pizza Dough (page 16)

¼ cup (½ stick) unsalted butter

1½ pounds fresh flavorful mushrooms such as chanterelle, morel, porcino, or shiitake, one type or a combination, sliced

½ cup dry sherry or port

2 tablespoons minced fresh thyme, or 2 teaspoons crumbled dried thyme

Salt

Freshly ground black pepper

Vegetable oil or cooking spray for greasing pizza screen or ventilated pizza pan

2 cups freshly shredded Gruyère cheese (about 8 ounces)

1 cup freshly shredded smoked Gouda, provolone, or other smoked cheese (about 4 ounces)

Truffle oil, extra-virgin olive oil, or walnut oil for brushing crust and drizzling over toppings

Pink pepperberries (dried fruit of *Schinus molle* tree) for garnish (optional)

Fresh thyme sprigs for garnish

Nowadays, those of us who enjoy flavorful mushrooms no longer have to forage the forests in search of the wild fungi. Many of these varieties are now being cultivated and are readily available. But the taste is still "wild" and exciting. For an interesting presentation, choose four different types and colors of flavorful mushrooms and cook each one separately. Divide the pizza into sections as described in the recipe for Four Seasons Pizza (page 38) and fill each section with a different mushroom.

Brushing the crust and drizzling the mushrooms with a little truffle-flavored olive oil adds to the earthy flavor.

If necessary, review Making Perfect Pizza at Home (pages 9–25).

Make the selected pizza dough and set aside to rise as directed.

In a sauté pan or skillet, melt the butter over medium-high heat. Add the mushrooms and cook, stirring frequently, until almost tender, about 3 minutes. Add the sherry or port, thyme, and salt and pepper to taste and continue cooking until the liquid is evaporated, 2 to 3 minutes longer. Transfer to a colander set over a bowl and set aside to drain well and cool to room temperature.

About 30 minutes before baking the pizza, prepare an oven as directed on page 21 and preheat it to 500 degrees F. Brush a pizza screen or ventilated pizza pan with vegetable oil or coat with spray and set aside. As this pizza must be removed from the oven before the crust is completely set, do not bake directly on a stone or tiles.

In a bowl, combine the Gruyère and smoked cheeses and set aside.

On a lightly floured surface, roll out or stretch the dough and shape it as desired. Place the dough on the prepared screen or pan. Prick the dough all over with a fork and brush it with truffle, olive, or walnut oil, then top with the cheese mixture, leaving a ½-inch border around the edges. Drizzle with truffle, olive, or walnut oil.

Transfer the pizza to the preheated oven and bake only until the crust is lightly browned, about 6 minutes.

Meanwhile, blot the mushrooms with paper toweling to remove excess moisture.

Remove the pizza to a work surface and quickly distribute the mushrooms over the cheese. Return to the oven and bake until the crust is golden and the cheese is bubbly, about 4 minutes longer.

Remove the pizza to a wire rack and let stand for about 2 minutes, then transfer to a cutting tray or board and lightly brush the edges of the crust with truffle, olive, or walnut oil. Sprinkle with the pepperberries (if using) and garnish with thyme sprigs. Slice and serve immediately.

Makes 8 servings

California-Style Pizza Dough (page 18) or Neapolitan-Style Pizza Dough (page 16)

Sun-Dried Tomato Pesto
1 tablespoon chopped garlic
1 cup chopped, drained sun-dried tomatoes packed in olive oil
½ cup freshly grated Parmesan cheese, preferably Parmigiano-Reggiano
½ cup fresh basil leaves
2 tablespoons oil from sun-dried tomatoes
Salt
Freshly ground black pepper

Vegetable oil or cooking spray for greasing pizza screen or ventilated pizza pan (if using)
Cornmeal for sprinkling pizza peel (if using)
Oil from sun-dried tomatoes for brushing crust
3 cups freshly shredded high-quality semisoft mozzarella cheese (about 9 ounces), preferably made with whole milk

Sun-Dried Tomato Pesto Pizza

This simple pie celebrates the rich summer flavor captured in sun-dried tomatoes. As the flavor is intense, you may prefer this pizza in small appetizer-sized wedges, or offer it with a salad of mixed greens as a main dish.

If necessary, review Making Perfect Pizza at Home (pages 9–25).

Make the selected pizza dough and set aside to rise as directed.

To make the Sun-Dried Tomato Pesto, in a food processor, combine the garlic and tomatoes and process as finely as possible. Add the Parmesan cheese, basil, and oil and process as smoothly as possible. Transfer to a small bowl and season to taste with salt and pepper.

About 30 minutes before baking the pizza, prepare an oven as directed on page 21 and preheat it to 500 degrees F. If using a pizza screen or ventilated pan, brush it with vegetable oil or coat with spray and set aside. If baking directly on a stone or tiles, sprinkle a pizza peel with cornmeal and set aside.

On a lightly floured surface, roll out or stretch the dough and shape it as desired. Place the dough on the prepared screen, pan, or peel. Brush the dough all over with oil from the sun-dried tomatoes, then spread with the tomato pesto, leaving a ½-inch border around the edges. Distribute the cheese over the pesto. If using a pizza peel, give it a quick, short jerk to be sure that the bottom of the crust has not stuck to it.

Transfer the pizza to the preheated oven and bake until the crust is golden, about 10 minutes.

Remove the pizza to a wire rack and let stand for about 2 minutes, then transfer to a cutting tray or board and lightly brush the edges of the crust with more of the tomato oil. Slice and serve immediately.

Makes 8 servings

2 pounds small beets

California-Style Pizza Dough (page 18) or Neapolitan-Style Pizza Dough (page 16)

2 cups tender, young beet greens or arugula

Vegetable oil or cooking spray for greasing pizza screen or ventilated pizza pan (if using)

Cornmeal for sprinkling pizza peel (if using)

1½ cups crumbled Roquefort or other blue cheese (about 6 ounces)

1½ cups freshly shredded Gruyère cheese (about 4½ ounces)

Extra-virgin olive oil for brushing beets and crust

Salt

Freshly ground black pepper

½ cup chopped toasted walnuts

The-Beet-Goes-On Pizza

Roasted beets are complemented by blue cheese on top of this only-in-California pizza. For a colorful topping, use a combination of beets in varying shades of red and gold. And don't forget to play Sonny and Cher songs while enjoying this richly flavored pie.

Prepare an oven as directed on page 21, position a rack in the middle of the oven for roasting the beets, and preheat the oven to 350 degrees F.

If the beets have tender greens attached, remove and reserve the greens for later use. Wash the beets under cold running water to remove all traces of soil, then pat dry with paper toweling. Trim off all but about 2 inches of the stem and root from each beet. Wrap the beets in aluminum foil. Place the foil packet(s) on a baking sheet, transfer to the preheated oven, and roast until the beets are easily pierced in their centers with a wooden skewer inserted through the foil, about 1½ hours.

Meanwhile, if necessary, review Making Perfect Pizza at Home (pages 9–25).

Make the selected pizza dough and set aside to rise as directed.

When the beets are done, unwrap and transfer them to a plate. When they are cool enough to handle, using your fingertips, peel off and discard the skins. Set the beets aside to cool to room temperature.

Remove and discard any tough stems from the beet greens or arugula and wash the leaves under cold running water. Place in a salad spinner and spin to remove as much water as possi-

ble. Pat dry with paper toweling. Wrap in a cloth kitchen towel or paper toweling and refrigerate for at least 30 minutes to crisp, or place the wrapped leaves in a plastic bag and refrigerate for up to several hours.

About 30 minutes before baking the pizza, preheat the oven to 500 degrees F. If using a pizza screen or ventilated pan, brush it with vegetable oil or coat with spray and set aside. If baking directly on a stone or tiles, sprinkle a pizza peel with cornmeal and set aside.

In a bowl, combine the blue and Gruyère cheeses and set aside.

Slice the beets about ¼ inch thick, brush the slices with olive oil, sprinkle with salt and pepper to taste, and set aside.

On a lightly floured surface, roll out or stretch the dough and shape it as desired. Place the dough on the prepared screen, pan, or peel. Brush the dough all over with olive oil, then cover with the cheese mixture, leaving a ½-inch border around the edges. Distribute the beet slices over the cheese. If using a pizza peel, give it a quick, short jerk to be sure that the bottom of the crust has not stuck to it.

Transfer the pizza to the preheated oven and bake until the crust is golden, about 10 minutes.

▶

Remove the pizza to a wire rack and let stand for about 2 minutes, then transfer to a cutting tray or board and lightly brush the edges of the crust with olive oil. Sprinkle with the toasted walnuts and top with the chilled beet greens or arugula. Slice and serve immediately.

Makes 8 servings

On the West Coast, most folks prefer a chewy crust flavored with olive oil and topped with a wide range of ingredients that make pizzeria chefs in Italy shake their heads in bewilderment.

California-Style Pizza Dough (page 18) or Neapolitan-Style Pizza Dough (page 16)

Vegetable oil or cooking spray for greasing pizza screen or ventilated pizza pan (if using)

Cornmeal for sprinkling pizza peel (if using)

2 cups freshly grated Parmesan cheese (about 8 ounces), preferably Parmigiano-Reggiano

5 ounces fresh soft mozzarella packed in water, preferably water-buffalo type from Italy, thinly sliced and cut into small pieces, or 2 cups freshly shredded high-quality semi-soft mozzarella cheese (about 6 ounces), preferably made with whole milk

Extra-virgin olive oil for brushing crust and drizzling over toppings

1 tablespoon minced fresh rosemary, or 1 teaspoon finely crumbled dried rosemary

2 cups finely chopped pistachios

3/4 cup finely chopped red onion

Salt

Freshly ground white pepper

Pistachio and Parmesan Pizza

The idea for this unusual pizza topping came from Pizzeria Bianco, housed in a charming brick building in the Heritage Square section of Phoenix, Arizona. In 1999, the pizzas served there were such a hit with the attendees at the annual conference of the International Association of Culinary Professionals that the place bulged for a full week with the who's who of the food world.

As there are so few ingredients, it is imperative that the pistachios be absolutely fresh and the cheese and oil of the highest quality. I've used both raw and roasted pistachios and both are good. If using roasted ones, watch carefully to prevent burning near the end of baking.

If necessary, review Making Perfect Pizza at Home (pages 9–25).

Make the selected pizza dough and set aside to rise as directed.

About 30 minutes before baking the pizza, prepare an oven as directed on page 21 and preheat it to 500 degrees F. If using a pizza screen or ventilated pan, brush it with vegetable oil or coat with spray and set aside. If baking directly on a stone or tiles, sprinkle a pizza peel with cornmeal and set aside.

In a bowl, combine the Parmesan and mozzarella cheeses and set aside.

On a lightly floured surface, roll out or stretch the dough and shape it as desired. Place the dough on the prepared screen, pan, or peel. Brush the dough all over with olive oil, then sprinkle with the rosemary. Top with the cheese mixture, leaving a 1/2-inch border around the edges. Distribute the pistachios and onion over the cheese and drizzle with olive oil. Sprinkle with salt and pepper to taste. If using a pizza peel, give it a quick,

short jerk to be sure that the bottom of the crust has not stuck to it.

Transfer the pizza to the preheated oven and bake until the crust is golden, about 10 minutes; watch carefully near the end to prevent the nuts from burning.

Remove the pizza to a wire rack and let stand for about 2 minutes, then transfer to a cutting tray or board and lightly brush the edges of the crust with olive oil. Slice and serve immediately.

Makes 8 servings

Caribbean Jerk Shrimp Pizza with Tropical Salsa

In Jamaica, *jerk* is the term applied to a style of spicy grilled foods. Although the shrimp are cooked on the pizza instead of a grill, they have the typical *jerk* flavor from the spicy marinade. Other seafood can be substituted for the shrimp. The fiery heat of the Jamaican chile is tempered by the cooling fruit in the salsa strewn over the pizza.

Jerk Paste

½ cup coarsely chopped yellow onion

1 tablespoon coarsely chopped fresh Scotch Bonnet or other hot chile, or to taste

¼ cup sliced green onion, including green tops

1½ teaspoons fresh thyme leaves, or ½ teaspoon crumbled dried thyme

½ teaspoon ground allspice

¼ teaspoon ground cinnamon

⅛ teaspoon freshly grated nutmeg

1 teaspoon salt

½ teaspoon freshly ground black pepper

Jamaican hot sauce (optional)

1 pound large shrimp, peeled and deveined

Tropical Salsa

1 cup finely diced ripe mango

1 cup finely diced ripe pineapple

½ cup minced green onion, including green tops

1 tablespoon minced fresh Scotch Bonnet or other hot chile, or to taste

½ cup minced fresh cilantro (coriander)

1 tablespoon unseasoned rice vinegar

Salt

California-Style Pizza Dough (page 18) or Neapolitan-Style Pizza Dough (page 16)

Vegetable oil or cooking spray for greasing pizza screen or ventilated pizza pan

1½ cups freshly shredded high-quality semisoft mozzarella cheese (about 4½ ounces), preferably made with whole milk

1½ cups freshly shredded white Cheddar cheese (about 4½ ounces)

Extra-virgin olive oil for brushing crust

To make the Jerk Paste, in a small food processor, combine all of the paste ingredients, including hot sauce to taste (if using), and blend as smoothly as possible. Transfer to a bowl.

Quickly rinse the shrimp under cold running water and pat dry with paper toweling. Add them to the bowl of Jerk Paste and turn to coat all over. Cover and refrigerate for at least 1 hour or for up to several hours; return to room temperature shortly before cooking.

To make the Tropical Salsa, in a small bowl, combine all of the salsa ingredients, including salt to taste. Cover and refrigerate for at least 1 hour or for up to several hours; return almost to room temperature before using.

If necessary, review Making Perfect Pizza at Home (pages 9–25).

Make the selected pizza dough and set aside to rise as directed.

About 30 minutes before baking the pizza, prepare an oven as directed on page 21 and preheat it to 500 degrees F. Brush a pizza screen or ventilated

▶

pan with vegetable oil or coat with spray and set aside. As this pizza must be removed from the oven before the crust is completely set, do not bake directly on a stone or tiles.

In a bowl, combine the mozzarella and Cheddar cheeses and set aside.

On a lightly floured surface, roll out or stretch the dough and shape it as desired. Place the dough on the prepared screen, pan, or peel. Brush the dough all over with olive oil, then cover with the cheese mixture, leaving a 1/2-inch border around the edges.

Transfer the pizza to the preheated oven and bake until the crust just begins to brown, about 5 minutes.

Remove the pizza from the oven and quickly arrange the shrimp over the top. Return to the oven and bake until the crust is golden and the shrimp turn opaque, about 5 minutes longer; do not overcook the shrimp.

Remove the pizza to a wire rack and let stand for about 2 minutes, then transfer to a cutting tray or board and lightly brush the edges of the crust with olive oil. Drain the salsa well and spoon it over the pizza. Slice and serve immediately.

Makes 8 servings

The average North American family enjoys pizza at home at least thirty times per year.

California-Style Pizza Dough (page 18; substitute canola or other bland vegetable oil for the olive oil) or Neapolitan-Style Pizza Dough (page 16)

Vegetable oil or cooking spray for greasing pizza screen or ventilated pizza pan

Canola or other bland vegetable oil for brushing crust and drizzling over toppings

1 pound Brie cheese, rind discarded, cut into small pieces

12 ounces thinly sliced smoked salmon, cut into small pieces

1/2 cup minced sweet onion

Fresh dill sprigs for garnish

Smoked Salmon and Brie Pizza

Serve this opulent concoction as an unusual addition to a brunch menu, or cut *pizzette* into small wedges and pass with drinks before dinner.

If necessary, review Making Perfect Pizza at Home (pages 9–25).

Make the selected pizza dough and set aside to rise as directed.

About 30 minutes before baking the pizza, prepare an oven as directed on page 21 and preheat it to 500 degrees F. Brush a pizza screen or ventilated pizza pan with vegetable oil or coat with spray and set aside. As this pizza must be removed from the oven before the crust is completely set, do not bake directly on a pizza stone or tiles.

On a lightly floured surface, roll out or stretch the dough and shape it as desired. Place the dough on the prepared screen or pan. Prick the dough all over with a fork, then brush it with vegetable oil.

Transfer the screen or pan to the preheated oven and bake until the crust just begins to brown, about 5 minutes.

Remove the screen or pan from the oven and top the crust with the cheese, leaving a 1/2-inch border around the edges. Distribute the salmon and onion over the cheese and drizzle evenly with vegetable oil. Return to the oven and bake until the crust is golden, about 5 minutes longer.

Remove the pizza to a wire rack and let stand for about 2 minutes, then transfer to a cutting tray or board and lightly brush the edges of the crust with oil. Garnish with dill. Slice and serve immediately.

Makes 8 servings

Coconut Marinade

¾ cup unsweetened coconut milk

2 tablespoons minced garlic

3 tablespoons minced fresh cilantro
(coriander), preferably roots or
lower stem portions

2 tablespoons fish sauce, preferably
Thai or Vietnamese

1 tablespoon soy sauce, preferably
dark Chinese style

1 teaspoon ground turmeric

1 teaspoon sugar

½ teaspoon freshly ground white
pepper

1½ pounds boned and skinned
chicken breast halves or thighs
(about 4 breast halves or 8
thighs)

Sweet Chile-Garlic Sauce

1 cup distilled white vinegar

½ cup sugar

1½ teaspoons salt

1½ teaspoons bottled Asian chile-
garlic sauce, or 1 teaspoon
minced fresh red chile and
½ teaspoon minced garlic

My Thai Pizza

In my first pizza book, I included a Thai-inspired chicken topping. Since that time, I have researched and written a book on Southeast Asian cooking and have learned much more about the ingredients of the region. Although there is no such dish in Thailand, here is an updated version of my Thai pizza. All it needs is a non-Thai mai tai or some Thai iced tea alongside.

Instead of using an oven as directed, the chicken can be cooked in a covered grill with moderate indirect heat. Both the chicken and the Sweet Chile-Garlic Sauce can be cooked up to a day ahead of making the pizza.

California-Style Pizza Dough (page
18; substitute roasted peanut
oil or Asian sesame oil for the
olive oil)

Vegetable oil or cooking spray for
greasing pizza screen or
ventilated pizza pan (if using)

Cornmeal for sprinkling pizza peel
(if using)

1½ cups freshly shredded high-
quality semisoft mozzarella
cheese (about 4½ ounces),
preferably made with whole
milk

1½ cups freshly shredded
Monterey Jack cheese
(about 4½ ounces)

Roasted peanut oil or hot chile oil
for brushing crust

1 cup bean sprouts

½ cup slivered carrot

½ cup chopped fresh cilantro
(coriander)

¼ cup thinly sliced green onion,
including green tops

¼ cup coarsely chopped dry-roasted
peanuts

To make the Coconut Marinade, in a nonreactive (glass, ceramic, or stainless steel) bowl, combine all of the marinade ingredients and mix well.

Quickly rinse the chicken under cold running water, pat dry with paper toweling, and add it to the marinade. Turn to coat well. Cover and refrigerate, turning the chicken several times, for about 4 hours; return the chicken to room temperature before cooking.

To make the Sweet Chile-Garlic Sauce, in a small saucepan, combine the vinegar, sugar, and salt. Place over medium-high heat and bring to a boil, stirring to dissolve the sugar and salt. Cook until the mixture is syrupy, about 15 minutes. Remove from the heat, stir in the chile-garlic sauce or chile and garlic, and set aside. (The sauce will thicken further as it cools.)

If necessary, review Making Perfect Pizza at Home (pages 9–25).

Make the California-Style Pizza Dough and set aside to rise as directed.

Prepare an oven as directed on page 21, position a rack in the middle of the oven for cooking the chicken, and preheat the oven to 350 degrees F.

Place the chicken and the marinade in a baking pan, cover with aluminum foil, transfer to the preheated oven, and bake until the chicken is tender and just opaque when cut into at the thickest part with a small, sharp knife, about 20 minutes for breasts or about 45 minutes for thighs.

Remove the pan from the oven, uncover, and set aside to cool. As soon as the chicken is cool enough to handle, transfer it to a work surface and reserve the pan juices. Shred or chop the chicken into very small pieces and transfer to a bowl. Drizzle the pan juices over the chicken and toss to coat well. Set aside to cool to room temperature, then cover and refrigerate until needed; return to room temperature and drain off any excess liquid before adding to the pizza.

About 30 minutes before baking the pizza, preheat the oven to 500 degrees F. If using a pizza screen or ventilated pan, brush it with vegetable oil or coat with spray and set aside. If baking directly on a stone or tiles, sprinkle a pizza peel with cornmeal and set aside.

In a bowl, combine the mozzarella and Monterey Jack cheeses and set aside.

On a lightly floured surface, roll out or stretch the dough and shape it as desired. Place the dough on the prepared screen, pan, or peel. Brush the dough all over with roasted peanut or hot chile oil, then top with the cheese mixture, leaving a ½-inch border around the edges. Distribute the chicken evenly over the cheese. If using a pizza peel, give it a quick, short jerk to be sure that the bottom of the crust has not stuck to it.

Transfer the pizza to the preheated oven and bake until the crust is golden, about 10 minutes.

Remove the pizza to a wire rack and let stand for about 2 minutes, then transfer to a cutting tray or board and lightly brush the edges of the crust with roasted peanut or hot chile oil. Sprinkle with the bean sprouts, carrot, cilantro, green onion, and peanuts. Slice and serve immediately. Pass the reserved Sweet Chile-Garlic Sauce at the table for drizzling over the pizza.

Makes 8 servings

Yogurt Marinade

1 cup plain yogurt

2 tablespoons freshly squeezed lime juice

2 tablespoons grated or minced fresh ginger

2 tablespoons minced garlic

1 tablespoon ground paprika

2 teaspoons ground *garam masala* (available in Indian markets)

1 teaspoon salt

1 teaspoon ground cayenne

Red and yellow food coloring (optional; see recipe introduction)

1½ pounds boned and skinned chicken breast halves or thighs (about 4 breast halves or 8 thighs)

California-Style Pizza Dough (page 18; substitute Asian sesame oil for the olive oil)

Vegetable oil or cooking spray for greasing pizza screen or ventilated pizza pan (if using)

Cornmeal for sprinkling pizza peel (if using)

Asian sesame oil or hot chile oil for brushing crust

3 cups freshly shredded Monterey Jack cheese (about 9 ounces)

½ cup sliced green onion, including green tops

Mango chutney for serving (a favorite recipe or high-quality commercial product)

Tandoori Pizza

India meets Italy or, more accurately, California, in this delightful combination. The pizza crust resembles nan (naan), the Indian bread cooked in the intense heat of tandoor ovens. Food coloring will give this spiced roasted chicken the traditional orange-red color of tandoor-cooked foods. A British-style mango chutney spread on the pizza adds some sweet relief to the spicy chicken.

To make the Yogurt Marinade, in a nonreactive (glass, ceramic, or stainless steel) bowl, combine the yogurt, lime juice, ginger, garlic, paprika, *garam masala,* salt, and cayenne and blend well. If desired, gradually blend in enough red and yellow food coloring to achieve a deep orange-red.

Rinse the chicken under cold running water, pat dry with paper toweling, and add it to the marinade. Turn to coat well. Cover and refrigerate for at least 4 hours or for up to overnight; return the chicken to room temperature before cooking.

If necessary, review Making Perfect Pizza at Home (pages 9–25).

Make the California-Style Pizza Dough and set aside to rise as directed.

Prepare an oven as directed on page 21, position a rack in the middle of the oven for roasting the chicken, and preheat the oven to 500 degrees F.

Place the chicken on a rack set in a shallow roasting pan. Transfer to the preheated oven and roast until the chicken is tender and just opaque when cut into at the thickest part with a small, sharp knife, about 10 minutes for breasts or about 20 minutes for thighs.

Remove the pan from the oven and set aside to cool. As soon as the chicken is cool enough to handle, chop the meat into small bite-sized pieces

and transfer to a bowl. Set aside to cool to room temperature, then cover and refrigerate until needed; return to room temperature before adding to the pizza.

About 30 minutes before baking the pizza, preheat the oven to 500 degrees F. If using a pizza screen or ventilated pan, brush it with vegetable oil or coat with spray and set aside. If baking directly on a stone or tiles, sprinkle a pizza peel with cornmeal and set aside.

On a lightly floured surface, roll out or stretch the dough and shape it as desired. Place the dough on the prepared screen, pan, or peel. Brush the dough all over with sesame or hot chile oil, then top with the cheese, leaving a ½-inch border around the edges. Distribute the chicken over the cheese and sprinkle with the green onion. If using a pizza peel, give it a quick, short jerk to be sure that the bottom of the crust has not stuck to it.

Transfer the pizza to the preheated oven and bake until the crust is golden, about 10 minutes.

Remove the pizza to a wire rack and let stand for about 2 minutes, then transfer to a cutting tray or board and lightly brush the edges of the crust with sesame or hot chile oil. Slice and serve immediately. Pass the chutney at the table for spooning over the pizza.

Makes 8 servings

Barbecued Chicken Pizza

Since the 1980s, I've been grateful to California Pizza Kitchen for introducing this totally American concept to the world of pizzas. Use your favorite made-from-scratch tomato-based barbecue sauce or any high-quality commercial sauce. If you prefer, cook the chicken in a covered grill using moderate indirect heat.

California-Style Pizza Dough (page
    18) or Whole-Wheat Pizza
    Dough (page 20)
1/4 cup sesame seed
2 garlic heads, separated into
    cloves, peeled, and coarsely
    chopped
2 teaspoons crushed dried chile
1/2 cup soy sauce
5 tablespoons honey
1 1/2 cups unseasoned rice vinegar
1/4 cup canola or other high-quality
    vegetable oil
1 1/2 pounds boned and skinned
    chicken breast halves (about
    4), cut into bite-sized pieces
Vegetable oil or cooking spray for
    greasing pizza screen or
    ventilated pizza pan (if using)
Cornmeal for sprinkling pizza peel
    (if using)
2 cups freshly shredded Gruyère
    cheese (about 8 ounces)
1 cup freshly shredded high-quality
    semisoft mozzarella cheese
    (about 3 ounces), preferably
    made with whole milk
Asian sesame oil for brushing crust
1/4 cup finely chopped green onion,
    including green tops

Garlic-Glazed Chicken Pizza

I hadn't made this pizza, which I created for my first pizza book, in years, and I'd forgotten how delicious it was. Since asked to bake it on a recent appearance on *Home Cooking with Amy Coleman,* a PBS television series, it has returned to a place of favor in my kitchen.

If necessary, review Making Perfect Pizza at Home (pages 9–25).

Make the selected pizza dough and set aside to rise as directed.

In a small skillet, place the sesame seed over medium heat and toast, shaking the pan or stirring frequently, until lightly golden and fragrant, about 5 minutes. Pour onto a plate to cool.

In a bowl, combine the garlic, chile, soy sauce, honey, and vinegar. Set aside.

In a large sauté pan or skillet, heat the 1/4 cup vegetable oil over medium-high heat. Add the chicken and cook, stirring frequently, until opaque on all sides, about 3 minutes. Using a slotted utensil, transfer the chicken to a plate and set aside. Pour the garlic mixture into the skillet and cook, stirring frequently, until the sauce is reduced to the consistency of syrup, about 15 minutes. Return the chicken pieces to the pan, and cook, stirring constantly, until the chicken is lightly glazed, about 2 minutes. Remove from the heat and set aside to cool to room temperature, then cover and refrigerate until needed; return to room temperature before adding to the pizza.

About 30 minutes before baking the pizza, prepare an oven as directed on page 21 and preheat it to 500 degrees F. If using a pizza screen or ventilated pan, brush it with vegetable oil or coat with spray and set aside. If baking directly on a stone or tiles, sprinkle a pizza peel with cornmeal and set aside.

In a bowl, combine the Gruyère and mozzarella cheeses and set aside.

On a lightly floured surface, roll out or stretch the dough and shape it as desired. Place the dough on the prepared screen, pan, or peel. Brush the dough all over with sesame oil, then top with the cheese mixture, leaving a 1/2-inch border around the edges. Distribute the chicken over the cheese. If using a pizza peel, give it a quick, short jerk to be sure that the bottom of the crust has not stuck to it.

Transfer the pizza to the preheated oven and bake until the crust is golden, about 10 minutes.

Remove the pizza to a wire rack and let stand for about 2 minutes, then transfer to a cutting tray or board and lightly brush the edges of the crust with sesame oil. Sprinkle with the green onion and toasted sesame seed. Slice and serve immediately.

Makes 8 servings

Oven Kalua Pig

2 pounds boneless pork shoulder
  roast (Boston butt)
2 tablespoons soy sauce
1½ tablespoons liquid smoke
1 tablespoon coarse salt, preferably
  Hawaiian rock salt
Pesticide-free banana, taro, ti, or
  spinach leaves

California-Style Pizza Dough
  (page 18)
Vegetable oil or cooking spray for
  greasing pizza screen or
  ventilated pizza pan (if using)
Cornmeal for sprinkling pizza peel
  (if using)
Extra-virgin olive oil for brushing
  crust
2 cups crumbled fresh mild goat
  cheese (about 8 ounces)
½ cup thinly sliced yellow onion,
  preferably a sweet variety
  such as Maui or Vidalia
2 tablespoons slivered fresh hot
  chile, or to taste
2 cups diced ripe mango or papaya
  tossed in 1 tablespoon freshly
  squeezed lime juice
¼ cup minced green onion, including green tops

Kalua Pig and Goat Cheese Pizza

This combination was inspired by a quesadilla that I enjoyed at Merriman's in Waimea on the Big Island of Hawaii. A smoky kalua pig is the focal point of a traditional Hawaiian *'aha'aina,* an out-door feast commonly called a luau. This oven version renders similar flavor without digging up the yard for an *imu,* a pit lined with hot rocks for cooking a whole pig. I wrap the pork in banana leaves, which I purchase frozen from Latin and Asian markets. Your local florist may be able to secure fresh banana or ti leaves. The pork can be cooked and refrigerated up to a day ahead.

Prepare an oven as directed on page 21, position a rack in the middle of the oven for cooking the pork, and preheat the oven to 525 degrees F.

To make the Oven Kalua Pig, quickly rinse the pork under cold running water, pat dry with paper toweling, and place on a sheet of heavy-duty aluminum foil that is large enough to later enclose the pork. Rub the soy sauce and liquid smoke over the pork to cover all sides. Sprinkle the meat all over with the salt. Wrap the pork with enough leaves to cover it completely, then bring up the sides of the foil to enclose the meat and seal tightly. Place the package in a baking pan, cover tightly with aluminum foil, transfer to the preheated oven, and bake for 30 minutes.

Reduce the oven temperature to 325 degrees F and continue baking until the meat is very tender and falling apart, about 3½ hours longer.

Meanwhile, if necessary, review Making Perfect Pizza at Home (pages 9–25).

Make the California-Style Pizza Dough and set aside to rise as directed.

When the pork is done, remove the pan to a work surface and uncover. Unwrap the pork in the pan, discard the foil and leaves, and leave the meat and juices in the pan. Set aside to cool. As soon as the meat is cool enough to handle, using your fingers, shred it into bite-sized pieces into a bowl, discarding any fat. Pour the pan juices over the meat and toss well. Cover and refrigerate until needed; return to room temperature and drain off the juices before adding to the pizza.

About 30 minutes before baking the pizza, pre-heat the oven to 500 degrees F. If using a pizza screen or ventilated pan, brush it with vegetable oil or coat with spray and set aside. If baking directly on a stone or tiles, sprinkle a pizza peel with cornmeal and set aside.

On a lightly floured surface, roll out or stretch the dough and shape it as desired. Place the dough on the prepared screen, pan, or peel. Brush the dough all over with olive oil, then top with the cheese, leaving a ½-inch border around the edges. Distribute the pork, onion, and chile over the cheese. If using a pizza peel, give it a quick, short jerk to be sure that the bottom of the crust has not stuck to it.

Transfer the pizza to the preheated oven and bake until the crust is golden, about 10 minutes.

Remove the pizza to a wire rack and let stand for about 2 minutes, then transfer to a cutting tray or board and lightly brush the edges of the crust with olive oil. Sprinkle with the mango or papaya and green onion. Slice and serve immediately.

Makes 8 servings

According to *The Guinness Book of World Records*, the largest baked pizza on record measured 12,159 square feet and was made in Norwood, South Africa, in 1990.

California-Style Pizza Dough (page 18) or Neapolitan-Style Pizza Dough (page 16)

1 cup Pizzeria-Style Tomato Sauce (page 138)

Vegetable oil or cooking spray for greasing pizza screen or ventilated pizza pan (if using)

Cornmeal for sprinkling pizza peel (if using)

1½ cups freshly shredded high-quality semisoft mozzarella cheese (about 4½ ounces), preferably made with whole milk

1½ cups freshly shredded Gruyère cheese (about 6 ounces)

Extra-virgin olive oil for brushing crust and drizzling over toppings

8 ounces Canadian bacon or baked ham, thinly sliced and cut into small pieces

2 cups drained, chopped fresh or canned crushed pineapple or pineapple chunks

Salt

Freshly ground black pepper

¼ cup thinly sliced green onion, including green tops

Pork and Pineapple Pizza

People either love or hate this popular topping combo served up in some guise at every all-American pizzeria. I fall into the group of adoring fans. Take your choice of smoked pork product—baked ham or Canadian bacon—and either fresh or canned pineapple. Andrew, the resident native of Hawaii in our home, prefers canned pineapple to most of the picked-too-early fresh ones that arrive on the mainland. If you can locate a good fresh pineapple, especially one from Maui or Tahiti, it will add a wonderful flavor to the pie.

If necessary, review Making Perfect Pizza at Home (pages 9–25).

Make the selected pizza dough and set aside to rise as directed.

Prepare the Pizzeria-Style Tomato Sauce as directed and set aside to cool to room temperature.

About 30 minutes before baking the pizza, prepare an oven as directed on page 21 and preheat it to 500 degrees F. If using a pizza screen or ventilated pan, brush it with vegetable oil or coat with spray and set aside. If baking directly on a stone or tiles, sprinkle a pizza peel with cornmeal and set aside.

In a bowl, combine the mozzarella and Gruyère cheeses and set aside.

On a lightly floured surface, roll out or stretch the dough and shape it as desired. Place the dough on the prepared screen, pan, or peel. Brush the dough all over with olive oil, then top with the cheese mixture, leaving a ¾-inch border around the edges. Spoon the tomato sauce over the cheese as evenly as possible. Arrange the Canadian bacon or ham over the sauce, top with

the pineapple, and drizzle with olive oil. Sprinkle with salt and pepper to taste. If using a pizza peel, give it a quick, short jerk to be sure that the bottom of the crust has not stuck to it.

Transfer the pizza to the preheated oven and bake until the crust is golden, about 10 minutes.

Remove the pizza to a wire rack and let stand for about 2 minutes, then transfer to a cutting tray or board and lightly brush the edges of the crust with olive oil. Sprinkle with the green onion. Slice and serve immediately.

Makes 8 servings.

California-Style Pizza Dough (page 18) or Neapolitan-Style Pizza Dough (page 16)

Seasoned Tomato Pulp (page 136), or 2 cups peeled, seeded, well-drained, and finely chopped ripe tomato (see page 12)

1 pound sliced bacon

Vegetable oil or cooking spray for greasing pizza screen or ventilated pizza pan (if using)

Cornmeal for sprinkling pizza peel (if using)

Extra-virgin olive oil for brushing crust (optional)

3 cups freshly shredded high-quality semisoft mozzarella cheese (about 9 ounces), preferably made with whole milk

4 cups shredded iceberg or romaine lettuce

3 tablespoons homemade or high-quality commercial mayonnaise

Salt

Freshly ground black pepper

BLT Pizza

A classic BLT sandwich is my favorite summer treat, and the bacon, lettuce, and tomato components work well on a pizza. You may prefer to serve this *piadina* style (see page 116), folding over individual-sized pizzas and eating them out of hand after the crisp bacon and mayonnaise-dressed lettuce are strewn over the hot tomato-topped pizza.

If necessary, review Making Perfect Pizza at Home (pages 9–25).

Make the selected pizza dough and set aside to rise as directed.

If using Seasoned Tomato Pulp, prepare as directed and set aside to cool to room temperature. If using fresh tomato, reserve for later use.

Heat a heavy skillet over high heat. Arrange as many of the bacon slices as will fit in a single layer and cook for 1 or 2 minutes. Reduce the heat to medium-low and cook, turning several times and draining off the excess fat into a bowl as it is rendered, until the bacon is crisp. Transfer the bacon to a wire rack set on a baking sheet to drain well and blot with paper toweling to remove excess surface fat. Cook the remaining bacon in the same way. When the bacon is cooled enough to handle, crumble it into a bowl and set aside. Reserve the bowl of bacon drippings for brushing the crust if desired.

About 30 minutes before baking the pizza, prepare an oven as directed on page 21 and preheat it to 500 degrees F. If using a pizza screen or ventilated pan, brush it with vegetable oil or coat with spray and set aside. If baking directly on a stone or tiles, sprinkle a pizza peel with cornmeal and set aside.

On a lightly floured surface, roll out or stretch the dough and shape it as desired. Place the dough on the prepared screen, pan, or peel. Brush the dough all over with some of the reserved bacon drippings or olive oil, then top with the cheese, leaving a 1/2-inch border around the edges. Distribute the tomato over the cheese. If using a pizza peel, give it a quick, short jerk to be sure that the bottom of the crust has not stuck to it.

Transfer the pizza to the preheated oven and bake until the crust is golden, about 10 minutes.

Meanwhile, in a bowl, toss the lettuce with the mayonnaise and season to taste with salt and pepper.

Remove the pizza to a wire rack and let stand for about 2 minutes, then transfer to a cutting tray or board and lightly brush the edges of the crust with bacon drippings or olive oil. Sprinkle the bacon over the pizza and top with the lettuce. Slice and serve immediately.

Makes 8 servings

California-Style Pizza Dough (page
    18) or Neapolitan-Style Pizza
    Dough (page 16)
Seasoned Tomato Pulp (page 136)
4 medium-sized ears corn, shucked
12 ounces andouille sausage, cut
    into ¼-inch-thick slices
½ cup finely chopped shallot
1 tablespoon minced garlic
Salt
Freshly ground black pepper
Vegetable oil or cooking spray for
    greasing pizza screen or
    ventilated pizza pan (if using)
Cornmeal for sprinkling pizza peel
    (if using)
Extra-virgin olive oil for brushing
    crust
3 cups freshly shredded white
    Cheddar or Monterey Jack
    cheese (about 9 ounces)
Crushed dried chile
3 tablespoons minced green onion,
    including green tops

Cajun Andouille Sausage, Tomato, and Corn Pizza

My Louisiana roots are evident in this pie. If you can't locate andouille, a spicy pork sausage popular in Louisiana Cajun cooking, substitute Polish kielbasa or other smoked pure pork sausage.

If necessary, review Making Perfect Pizza at Home (pages 9–25).

Make the selected pizza dough and set aside to rise as directed.

Prepare the Seasoned Tomato Pulp as directed and set aside to cool to room temperature.

Rest the base of an ear of corn on a large, deep plate or inside a large bowl. With a sharp knife, cut down the length of the cob from the tip to the base. Leave behind a bit of pulp to avoid mixing tough corn fibers into the corn. Rotate the ear until you have stripped it of kernels. Turn the knife blade over and scrape the cob with the blunt edge to remove the pulp and milky juices. Repeat with the remaining ears of corn. There should be about 2 cups kernels. Set aside.

In a sauté pan or heavy skillet, place the sausage over medium-high heat and cook, stirring frequently, until the sausage fat is rendered and the meat is lightly browned, about 5 minutes. Using a slotted utensil, transfer the sausage to paper toweling to drain well and set aside to cool to room temperature.

Discard all but 2 tablespoons of the drippings from the pan in which the sausage was cooked. Place the pan over medium-low heat, add the corn and shallot and cook, stirring frequently, until the corn is tender, about 4 minutes for young corn, or up to 8 minutes for older corn. Stir in the garlic, season to taste with salt and pepper, and set aside to cool to room temperature.

About 30 minutes before baking the pizza, prepare an oven as directed on page 21 and preheat it to 500 degrees F. If using a pizza screen or ventilated pan, brush it with vegetable oil or coat with spray and set aside. If baking directly on a stone or tiles, sprinkle a pizza peel with cornmeal and set aside.

On a lightly floured surface, roll out or stretch the dough and shape it as desired. Place the dough on the prepared screen, pan, or peel. Brush the dough all over with olive oil, then top with the cheese, leaving a ½-inch border around the edges. Spoon the tomato pulp and corn-shallot mixture over the cheese, then arrange the sausage slices on top. Sprinkle with crushed chile to taste. If using a pizza peel, give it a quick, short

jerk to be sure that the bottom of the crust has
not stuck to it.

Transfer the pizza to the preheated oven and bake
until the crust is golden, about 10 minutes.

Remove the pizza to a wire rack and let stand for
about 2 minutes, then transfer to a cutting tray or
board and lightly brush the edges of the crust
with olive oil. Sprinkle with the green onion. Slice
and serve immediately.

Makes 8 servings

**In the United States,
commercial pizza sales
exceed $20 billion a year.**

Neapolitan-Style Pizza Dough
(page 16) or California-Style
Pizza Dough (page 18)
¼ cup olive oil
3 pounds yellow or white onions,
thinly sliced
Salt
Freshly ground black pepper
12 ounces hot or sweet Italian
sausage, cut into ¼-inch-thick
slices
1 tablespoon minced garlic
½ cup dry white wine
3 tablespoons chopped fresh flat-
leaf parsley
1 tablespoon minced fresh sage, or
1 teaspoon crumbled dried sage
Vegetable oil or cooking spray for
greasing pizza screen or
ventilated pizza pan (if using)
Cornmeal for sprinkling pizza peel
(if using)
1½ cups freshly shredded Italian
Fontina cheese (about
7½ ounces)
1½ cups freshly shredded high-
quality semisoft mozzarella
cheese (about 4½ ounces),
preferably made with whole
milk
½ cup freshly grated Parmesan
cheese (about 2 ounces),
preferably Parmigiano-
Reggiano
Extra-virgin olive oil for brushing
crust
1 tablespoon minced red sweet
pepper
1 tablespoon minced fresh flat-leaf
parsley

Caramelized Onion and Sausage Pizza

Onions slowly cooked until sweetly caramelized play off against zesty sausage in this full-flavored topping, one of my favorites. Take your choice of hot or sweet Italian sausage, or substitute any favorite upscale sausage made from chicken, duck, lamb, or other "gourmet" ingredients.

If necessary, review Making Perfect Pizza at Home (pages 9–25).

Make the selected pizza dough and set aside to rise as directed.

Meanwhile, in a large, heavy pan, heat the ¼ cup olive oil over medium heat. Add the onions and toss well to coat with the oil. Sprinkle generously with salt and pepper. Cover, reduce the heat to medium-low, and cook, stirring occasionally, until the onions are soft and lightly colored, about 30 minutes. Uncover, increase the heat to medium, and cook, stirring frequently, until the onions are very tender and well caramelized, 25 minutes or longer, depending on the moisture content of onions.

Add the sausage slices and garlic to the onions. Increase the heat to high, stir in the wine, chopped parsley, and sage and cook, stirring frequently, until the wine is reduced but the mixture is still moist, about 3 minutes. Remove from the heat and set aside to cool to room temperature.

About 30 minutes before baking the pizza, pre-pare an oven as directed on page 21 and preheat it to 500 degrees F. If using a pizza screen or ventilated pan, brush it with vegetable oil or coat with spray and set aside. If baking directly on a stone or tiles, sprinkle a pizza peel with cornmeal and set aside.

In a bowl, combine the Fontina and mozzarella cheeses and ¼ cup of the Parmesan cheese and set aside.

On a lightly floured surface, roll out or stretch the dough and shape it as desired. Place the dough on the prepared screen, pan, or peel. Brush the dough all over with olive oil, then top with the cheese mixture, leaving a ½-inch border around the edges. Distribute the onion-sausage mixture over the cheeses. If using a pizza peel, give it a quick, short jerk to be sure that the bottom of the crust has not stuck to it.

Transfer the pizza to the preheated oven and bake until the crust is golden, about 10 minutes.

Remove the pizza to a wire rack and let stand for about 2 minutes, then transfer to a cutting tray or board and lightly brush the edges of the crust with olive oil. Sprinkle with the remaining ¼ cup Parmesan cheese, the sweet pepper, and the minced parsley. Slice and serve immediately.

Makes 8 servings

Neapolitan-Style Pizza Dough (page 16) or California-Style Pizza Dough (page 18)

1 cup Pizzeria-Style Tomato Sauce (page 138)

Italian Meatballs

½ cup fresh bread crumbs

2 tablespoons milk

8 ounces ground lean beef

8 ounces ground lean pork or veal

1 egg

2 tablespoons minced yellow onion

1 teaspoon minced garlic

2 tablespoons minced fresh flat-leaf parsley

1 tablespoon minced fresh oregano, or 1 teaspoon crumbled dried oregano

1 teaspoon salt

½ teaspoon freshly ground black pepper

¼ cup extra-virgin olive oil

2 red sweet peppers, stems, seeds, and membranes discarded, then sliced into narrow strips

1 large yellow onion, sliced thinly

Vegetable oil or cooking spray for greasing pizza screen or ventilated pizza pan (if using)

Cornmeal for dusting pizza peel (if using)

Extra-virgin olive oil for brushing crust

3 cups freshly shredded provolone cheese (about 9 ounces)

Freshly grated Parmesan cheese

Crushed dried chile for serving

Meatball, Onion, and Pepper Pizza

During the years that I lived in New York City, I occasionally indulged in a robust sandwich of meatballs, grilled onions, sweet peppers, and provolone cheese on an Italian roll. Here are all those hearty flavors captured on a pizza. It can also be prepared deep-dish style or as a calzone (see page 23). Just add a glass of Zinfandel and enjoy a taste of New York's Little Italy.

If necessary, review Making Perfect Pizza at Home (pages 9–25).

Make the selected pizza dough and set aside to rise as directed.

Prepare the Pizzeria-Style Tomato Sauce as directed and set aside to cool to room temperature.

To make the Italian Meatballs, in a bowl, combine the bread crumbs and milk and set aside for a few minutes for the bread to soften. When the bread is soft, mash it with a fork. Add the beef, pork or veal, egg, onion, garlic, parsley, oregano, salt, and pepper. Handling the mixture as little as possible to avoid compacting the meat, mix well, then form the mixture into balls about 1 inch in diameter.

In a heavy sauté pan or skillet, heat the ¼ cup olive oil over medium-high heat. Carefully add as many of the meatballs as will fit in a single layer without crowding. Cook, turning as necessary, just until browned all over; they should still be slightly pink when cut into with a small, sharp knife. Using a slotted utensil, transfer the meatballs to a rack set on a baking sheet to drain well. Cook any remaining meatballs in the same way.

Reserve the oil remaining in the pan.

Add the sweet peppers and onion to the same pan used for browning the meatballs. Place over medium heat and cook, stirring frequently, until soft and golden, about 12 minutes. Remove from the heat and set aside to cool to room temperature.

Transfer the drained meatballs to the tomato sauce, toss to blend well, cover, and refrigerate until needed; return to room temperature before using.

About 30 minutes before baking the pizza, prepare an oven as directed on page 21 and preheat it to 500 degrees F. If using a pizza screen or ventilated pan, brush it with vegetable oil or coat with spray and set aside. If baking directly on a stone or tiles, sprinkle a pizza peel with cornmeal and set aside.

On a lightly floured surface, roll out or stretch the dough and shape it as desired. Place the dough on the prepared screen, pan, or peel. Brush the dough all over with olive oil, then top with the provolone cheese, leaving a ½-inch border around the edges. Spoon the meatballs and sauce over the cheese and scatter the pepper and

▶

onion mixture over the top. If using a pizza peel, give it a quick, short jerk to be sure that the bottom of the crust has not stuck to it.

Transfer the pizza to the preheated oven and bake until the crust is golden, about 10 minutes.

Remove the pizza to a wire rack and let stand for about 2 minutes, then transfer to a cutting tray or board and lightly brush the edges of the crust with olive oil. Slice and serve immediately. Pass the Parmesan cheese and chile at the table for sprinkling over the pizza.

Makes 8 servings

The annual per capita pizza consumption in the United States is twenty-three pounds.

Cornmeal Pizza Dough (page 20)

Chili con Carne
2 tablespoons canola or other high-
    quality vegetable oil
1 cup finely chopped white or yellow
    onion
1½ pounds ground round or other
    lean beef
1½ teaspoons minced garlic
¼ cup all-purpose flour
6 tablespoons ground dried ancho,
    pasilla, or other mild to medium-
    hot chile
1½ teaspoons ground cumin, or
    to taste
Salt
Freshly ground black pepper
1½ cups tomato sauce (a favorite
    recipe or high-quality commer-
    cial product)

1½ cups freshly shredded yellow
    Cheddar cheese (about
    4½ ounces)
1½ cups freshly shredded Monterey
    Jack cheese (about
    4½ ounces)
Olive oil for brushing pan and crust
½ cup minced red sweet onion
3 tablespoons chopped fresh
    cilantro (coriander)

Chili con Carne Deep-Dish Pizza

**Very popular in Texas, chili-topped pizza can be made mild to fiery to suit your taste. For a vegetar-
ian pizza, substitute about 4 cups of your favorite vegetarian chili in place of the Chili con Carne.**

If necessary, review Making Perfect Pizza at Home (pages 9–25).

Make the Cornmeal Pizza Dough and set aside to rise as directed.

To make the Chili con Carne, in a heavy stew pot, heat the vegetable oil over medium heat. Add the onion and cook until soft but not browned, about 5 minutes. Add the beef and garlic and cook, stirring constantly and breaking up the meat, until the beef is just past the pink stage, about 5 minutes. Add the flour, chile, cumin, and salt and pepper to taste. Stir in the tomato sauce, adjust the heat to maintain a simmer, and simmer, uncovered, until thickened and the flavors are well blended, about 30 minutes. Add a little water to the pot any time during the cooking if the mixture begins to dry out. Remove from the heat and set aside to cool to room temperature.

In a bowl, combine the Cheddar and Monterey Jack cheeses and set aside.

Prepare an oven as directed for deep-dish pizza on page 21 and preheat it to 475 degrees F. Brush a 15-inch deep-dish pizza pan or two 9-inch pans with olive oil.

Place the ball of dough in the 15-inch pan, or divide the dough into 2 equal pieces and place each in a 9-inch pan. Starting in the middle, press the dough with your fingertips to cover the bottom and about 1 inch up the sides of the pan(s), making the dough thickness as even as possible. Prick the bottom of the dough every ½ inch with a fork. Transfer the pan(s) to the bottom rack of the preheated oven and bake for 4 minutes.

Remove the pan(s) from the oven and lightly brush the crust(s) all over with olive oil. Quickly spread half of the cheese mixture completely over the bottom of the crust(s), dividing evenly if using 2 pans. Spoon the chili over the cheese, then sprinkle with the onion and cover with the remaining cheese mixture.

Return the pan(s) to the bottom rack of the oven and bake for 5 minutes, then move the pan(s) to a rack in the upper portion of the oven and bake until the crust is golden and the toppings are bubbly, about 15 minutes longer.

Remove the pan(s) to a wire rack and let stand for about 5 minutes. If baked in a pan with a removable bottom, remove the pizza and transfer to a cutting tray or board. Lightly brush the edges of the crust(s) with olive oil. Sprinkle with the cilantro. Slice and serve immediately.

Makes 8 servings

California-Style Pizza Dough (page 18) or Neapolitan-Style Pizza Dough (page 16)

2 pounds Swiss chard, mustard or turnip greens, or spinach, one type or a combination

1 tablespoon unsalted butter

1 tablespoon extra-virgin olive oil

1 cup finely chopped white or yellow onion

Salt

Freshly ground black pepper

1½ cups freshly shredded high-quality semisoft mozzarella cheese (about 4½ ounces), preferably made with whole milk

1½ cups freshly shredded white Cheddar cheese (about 4½ ounces)

Extra-virgin olive oil for brushing pan and crust

6 ounces thinly sliced flavorful baked ham, cut into narrow strips

8 eggs, at room temperature

Greens, Eggs, and Ham Deep-Dish Pizza

Thank you, Dr. Seuss, for the title inspiration of this great brunch or supper dish.

If necessary, review Making Perfect Pizza at Home (pages 9–25).

Make the selected pizza dough and set aside to rise as directed.

Wash the greens thoroughly and discard any tough stems. Transfer the damp leaves to a large sauté pan or heavy skillet and place over medium heat. Cook, stirring frequently, just until the greens are wilted and turn bright green, 3 to 5 minutes. Transfer to a colander to drain and use your hands to squeeze out as much moisture as possible. Transfer to a cutting surface and chop finely, then place in a bowl and set aside.

In the sauté pan or skillet, melt the butter with the 1 tablespoon olive oil over medium heat. Add the onion and cook, stirring frequently, until soft but not browned, about 5 minutes. Transfer to the bowl of greens, season to taste with salt and pepper, mix well, and set aside to cool.

In a bowl, combine the mozzarella and Cheddar cheeses and set aside.

Prepare an oven as directed for deep-dish pizza on page 21 and preheat it to 475 degrees F. Brush a 15-inch deep-dish pizza pan or two 9-inch pans with olive oil.

Place the ball of dough in the 15-inch pan, or divide the dough into 2 equal pieces and place each in a 9-inch pan. Starting in the middle, press the dough with your fingertips to cover the bottom and about 1 inch up the sides of the pan(s), making the dough thickness as even as possible. Prick the bottom of the dough every ½ inch with a fork. Transfer the pan(s) to the bottom rack of the preheated oven and bake for 4 minutes.

Remove the pan(s) from the oven and lightly brush the crust(s) all over with olive oil. Quickly spread half of the cheese mixture completely over the bottom of the crust(s), dividing evenly if using 2 pans. Distribute the ham and greens over the cheese. Using your fingertips, hollow out 8 indentations in the greens and cheese. Break the eggs one at a time into a cup and transfer one to each of the indentations. Sprinkle the eggs with salt and pepper to taste. Sprinkle the remaining cheese mixture over the top.

Return the pan(s) to the bottom rack of the oven and bake for 5 minutes, then move the pan(s) to a rack in the upper portion of the oven and bake until the crust is golden, about 15 minutes longer.

Remove the pan(s) to a wire rack and let stand for about 5 minutes. If baked in a pan with a removable bottom, remove the pizza and transfer to a cutting tray or board. Lightly brush the edges of the crust(s) with olive oil. Slice and serve immediately.

Makes 8 servings

California-Style Pizza Dough (page 18) or Cornmeal Pizza Dough (page 20)

2 tablespoons extra-virgin olive oil

1 cup finely chopped white or yellow onion

1 cup finely chopped red sweet pepper

2 teaspoons minced garlic

1 pound ground lean beef

1½ cups peeled, seeded, drained, and chopped ripe or canned tomato

½ cup raisins

½ teaspoon ground cumin

¼ teaspoon ground cloves

1 tablespoon red wine vinegar

½ cup slivered blanched almonds

Salt

Freshly ground black pepper

Vegetable oil or cooking spray for greasing pizza screen or ventilated pizza pan (if using)

Cornmeal for sprinkling pizza peel (if using)

1½ cups freshly shredded white Cheddar cheese (about 4½ ounces)

1½ cups crumbled fresh mild goat cheese (about 4 ounces)

Extra-virgin olive oil for brushing crust

40 small pimiento-stuffed green olives

Pizza, South American Way

The inspiration for the name of this pie came from one of my favorite Carmen Miranda songs, and the inspiration for the topping came from one of my favorite dishes, *picadillo*, a spicy yet sweet beef dish popular throughout Central and South America.

If necessary, review Making Perfect Pizza at Home (pages 9–25).

Make the selected pizza dough and set aside to rise as directed.

In a heavy sauté pan or skillet, heat the 2 tablespoons olive oil over medium-high heat. Add the onion and sweet pepper and cook, stirring frequently, until soft but not browned, about 5 minutes. Stir in the garlic and cook about 1 minute longer. Add the beef and cook, stirring constantly and breaking up the meat with a spoon, until the meat is just past the pink stage, about 3 minutes. Stir in the tomato, raisins, cumin, cloves, and vinegar. Reduce the heat to medium and cook, stirring frequently, until the mixture is almost dry, 5 to 10 minutes. Stir in the almonds, season to taste with salt and pepper, and set aside to cool completely.

About 30 minutes before baking the pizza, prepare an oven as directed on page 21 and preheat it to 500 degrees F. If using a pizza screen or ventilated pan, brush it with vegetable oil or coat with spray and set aside. If baking directly on a stone or tiles, sprinkle a pizza peel with cornmeal and set aside.

In a bowl, combine the Cheddar and goat cheeses and set aside.

On a lightly floured surface, roll out or stretch the dough and shape it as desired. Place the dough on the prepared screen, pan, or peel. Brush the dough all over with olive oil, then top with the cheese mixture, leaving a ½-inch border around the edges. Spoon the beef mixture over the cheese and scatter the olives over the top. If using a pizza peel, give it a quick, short jerk to be sure that the bottom of the crust has not stuck to it.

Transfer the pizza to the preheated oven and bake until the crust is golden, about 10 minutes.

Remove the pizza to a wire rack and let stand for about 2 minutes, then transfer to a cutting tray or board and lightly brush the edges of the crust with olive oil. Slice and serve immediately.

Makes 8 servings

Both classic and contemporary fillings can be encased by a crust in several versions of stuffed pizza. Traditional guises include double-crust pies, deep-fried pizza pockets, and the popular calzone. For appetizers or snacks, I have included spiral-rolled pizzas cut into pinwheels. Finally, there is the *piadina*-style pizza, topped with salad or meat after baking, folded over, and eaten like a sandwich.

Stuffed
Pizzas

California-Style Pizza Dough
  (page 18)
1 cup Pizzeria-Style Tomato Sauce
  (page 138)
2 pounds zucchini or other summer
  squash, finely chopped or
  shredded
Salt
2 tablespoons extra-virgin olive oil
1 cup finely chopped white or yellow
  onion
5 ounces pancetta (unsmoked Italian
  bacon), finely diced
2 teaspoons minced garlic
2½ cups freshly shredded Bel
  Paese, Fontina, or high-quality
  semisoft mozzarella cheese
  (about 7½ ounces), preferably
  made with whole milk
Freshly ground black pepper
Extra-virgin olive oil for brushing pan
  and crust
⅓ cup freshly grated Parmesan
  cheese (about 1½ ounces),
  preferably Parmigiano-
  Reggiano
Crushed dried chile
3 tablespoons minced fresh flat-leaf
  parsley

Zucchini-Stuffed Deep-Dish Pizza, Chicago Style

If you like, you can use Cornmeal Pizza Dough (page 20), which is typically used for single-crust deep-dish pies. Most Chicago pizzerias, however, favor plain Sicilian-style dough containing olive oil, similar to my California-style dough, for stuffed pizzas, which are thinner-crusted pies. For a vegetarian pie, omit the pancetta.

If necessary, review Making Perfect Pizza at Home (pages 9–25).

Make the California-Style Pizza Dough and set aside to rise as directed.

Prepare the Pizzeria-Style Tomato Sauce and set aside to cool to room temperature.

Place the squash in a colander set over a bowl or in a sink, sprinkle with salt, toss to distribute the salt, and let stand for about 30 minutes to draw out excess moisture.

Gently squeeze the squash to release as much moisture as possible. (First rinse the squash under cold running water if you wish to rid it of excess salt.) Set aside.

In a large sauté pan or skillet, heat the 2 table-spoons olive oil over medium-high heat. Add the onion and pancetta and cook, stirring frequently, until the onion is soft but not browned and the meat is translucent, about 5 minutes. Add the zucchini and garlic and cook, stirring frequently, until the zucchini is tender, 5 to 10 minutes longer. Set aside to cool completely, then add the

shredded cheese and mix well. Season to taste with salt and pepper and set aside.

Prepare an oven as directed for deep-dish pizza on page 21 and preheat it to 475 degrees F. Brush a 12-inch deep-dish pizza pan with olive oil.

Reserve one-third of the dough in the oiled rising bowl and cover with plastic wrap to prevent drying out. Place the larger portion of the dough into the prepared pan. Starting in the middle, press the dough with your fingertips to cover the bottom and about 1 inch up the sides of the pan, making the dough thickness as even as possible. Prick the bottom of the dough every ½ inch with a fork. Brush the dough all over with olive oil. Fill the dough shell with the reserved zucchini mixture.

Roll out or stretch the reserved dough portion into a 12-inch round. Center it over the filling and press the edges of the crusts together to seal. Cut a 1-inch slit in the center of the top crust to allow steam to escape during cooking, then gently press the top crust down over the filling. Brush the top all over with olive oil.

▶

Place the pan on the bottom rack of the pre-heated oven and bake for 10 minutes, then move the pan to a rack in the upper portion of the oven and bake until the crust is golden brown, about 10 minutes longer.

Remove the pan from the oven and spoon the tomato sauce over the top of the pie, then sprinkle with the Parmesan cheese and crushed chile to taste. Return to the rack in the upper portion of the oven and bake until the cheese is melted, about 5 minutes longer.

Remove the pan to a wire rack and let stand for about 5 minutes. If baked in a pan with a removable bottom, remove the pizza and transfer to a cutting tray or board. Lightly brush the edges of the crust with olive oil. Sprinkle with the parsley. Slice and serve immediately.

Makes 8 servings

Midwesterners lean toward deep-dish pizzas, known as Chicago style, with thick crusts that often contain cornmeal and are piled high with toppings.

Neapolitan-Style Pizza Dough
(page 16)

Roasted Tomatoes (page 137), or 2
cups peeled, seeded, well-
drained, and chopped ripe
tomato (see page 12)

2 tablespoons extra-virgin olive oil

1½ cups chopped white or yellow
onion

1 teaspoon minced garlic

1 tablespoon minced fresh oregano,
or 1 teaspoon crumbled dried
oregano

2 flat anchovy fillets, chopped

6 ounces thinly sliced prosciutto,
chopped or slivered

6 ounces thinly sliced mild salami,
chopped or slivered

½ cup high-quality fresh ricotta
cheese (about 4 ounces)

½ cup freshly shredded Italian
caciocavallo or Fontina cheese
(about 2½ ounces)

¼ cup chopped fresh flat-leaf
parsley

¼ teaspoon crushed dried chile, or
to taste

Salt

Freshly ground black pepper

Vegetable oil or cooking spray for
greasing pizza screen or
ventilated pizza pan (if using)

Cornmeal for sprinkling pizza peel
(if using)

Extra-virgin olive oil for brushing
crust

Stuffed Pizza, Palermo Style (*Sfincione*)

In the Sicilian city of Palermo, *sfincione* are both thick-crusted, flat pizzas with hearty toppings and their double-crusted, generously packed kin. The stuffed versions, which have roots in the meat-filled pies of the Middle East, are the likely inspiration for the popular Chicago-style deep-dish pizza (see page 111). This pie is very filling, so small portions are in order.

If necessary, review Making Perfect Pizza at Home (pages 9–25).

Make the Neapolitan-Style Pizza Dough and set aside to rise as directed.

If using Roasted Tomatoes, prepare as directed, chop coarsely, and set aside to cool to room temperature. If using fresh tomato, reserve for later use.

In a sauté pan or skillet, heat the 2 tablespoons olive oil over medium-high heat. Add the onion and cook, stirring frequently, until soft and golden, about 8 minutes. Stir in the garlic and cook about 1 minute longer. Add the tomato, oregano, and anchovies. Adjust the heat to maintain a simmer and cook, stirring occasionally, until the mixture is thickened, about 20 minutes. Transfer to a bowl to cool slightly, then add the chopped or slivered meats, the cheeses, parsley, and chile. Season to taste with salt and pepper and mix gently. Set aside to cool to room temperature.

About 30 minutes before baking the pizza, prepare an oven as directed on page 21 and preheat it to 500 degrees F. If using a pizza screen or ventilated pan, brush it with vegetable oil or coat with spray and set aside. If baking directly on a stone or tiles, sprinkle a pizza peel with cornmeal and set aside.

Divide the dough into 2 equal pieces. On a lightly floured surface, roll out or stretch 1 piece of the dough into a round about 10 inches in diameter. Place the dough on the prepared screen, pan, or peel. Brush the dough with olive oil, leaving a ½-inch border around the edges, then top with the meat-cheese mixture, leaving the border uncovered.

Roll out or stretch the second piece of dough into the same-sized round. Place the dough over the filling and pinch the edges of the 2 rounds of dough together to seal tightly. Brush the top evenly with olive oil. Cut a 1-inch slit in the center for steam to escape during baking. If using a pizza peel, give it a quick, short jerk to be sure that the bottom of the crust has not stuck to it.

Transfer the pizza to the oven and bake until the crust is golden and puffy, about 10 minutes.

Remove the pizza to a wire rack and let stand for about 2 minutes, then transfer to a cutting tray or board and lightly brush the crust with olive oil. Slice and serve warm or at room temperature.

Makes 8 servings

Neapolitan-Style Pizza Dough
(page 16)

2 pounds spinach

1 tablespoon unsalted butter

1 tablespoon extra-virgin olive oil

1 cup finely chopped white or yellow
onion

1 teaspoon minced garlic

2 cups crumbled high-quality feta
cheese (about 8 ounces)

1 tablespoon grated or minced fresh
lemon zest

Salt

Freshly ground black pepper

Extra-virgin olive oil for brushing pan
and crust

1 cup freshly grated kasseri cheese
(about 4 ounces), preferably
imported from Greece and
made from sheep's or goat's
milk, or Parmesan cheese,
preferably Parmigiano-
Reggiano

Spanakopizza

My riff on Greek *spanakopita,* the traditional pie of spinach or other greens mixed with cheese and encased in phyllo, uses pizza crust instead of phyllo. To avoid a soggy crust, squeeze out as much moisture as possible from the spinach.

If necessary, review Making Perfect Pizza at Home (pages 9–25).

Make the Neapolitan-Style Pizza Dough and set aside to rise as directed.

Wash the spinach carefully to remove any sand or grit and discard any tough stems. Transfer the damp spinach to a large sauté pan or heavy skillet and place over medium heat. Cook, stirring frequently, just until the spinach is wilted and turns bright green, 3 to 5 minutes. Transfer to a colander to drain and use your hands to squeeze out as much moisture as possible. Transfer to a cutting surface and chop finely, then place in a bowl and set aside.

In the sauté pan or skillet, melt the butter with the 1 tablespoon olive oil over medium heat. Add the onion and cook, stirring frequently, until soft but not browned, about 5 minutes. Stir in the garlic and cook about 1 minute longer. Transfer to the bowl of spinach and let the mixture cool completely, then stir in the feta cheese and lemon zest and mix well. Season to taste with salt and pepper. Set aside.

Prepare an oven as directed for deep-dish pizza on page 21 and preheat it to 475 degrees F. Brush a 12-inch deep-dish pizza pan with olive oil.

Reserve one-third of the dough in the oiled rising bowl and cover with plastic wrap to prevent drying out. Place the larger portion of the dough into the prepared pan. Starting in the middle, press the dough with your fingertips to cover the bottom and about 1 inch up the sides of the pan, making the dough thickness as even as possible. Prick the bottom of the dough every ½ inch with a fork. Brush the dough all over with olive oil. Sprinkle the dough shell with half of the kasseri or Parmesan cheese. Add the reserved spinach-feta mixture, then sprinkle with the remaining kasseri or Parmesan cheese.

Roll out or stretch the reserved dough portion into a 12-inch round. Center it over the filling and press the edges of the crusts together to seal. Cut a 1-inch slit in the center of the top crust to allow steam to escape during cooking, then gently press the top crust down over the filling. Brush the top all over with olive oil.

Place the pan on the bottom rack of the preheated oven and bake for 10 minutes, then move the pan to a rack in the upper portion of the oven and bake until the crust is golden brown, about 15 minutes longer.

Remove the pan to a wire rack and let stand for about 5 minutes. If baked in a pan with a removable bottom, remove the pizza and transfer to a cutting tray or board. Lightly brush the crust with olive oil. Slice and serve immediately.

Makes 8 servings

Seasoned Tomato Pulp (page 136) or
Roasted Tomatoes (page 137)

California-Style Pizza Dough (page
18) or Neapolitan-Style Pizza
Dough (page 16)

2 cups freshly shredded high-quality
semisoft mozzarella cheese
(about 6 ounces), preferably
made with whole milk

2 cups high-quality fresh ricotta
cheese (about 1 pound)

1/2 cup freshly grated Parmesan
cheese (about 2 ounces),
preferably Parmigiano-
Reggiano

Vegetable oil or cooking spray for
greasing pizza screen or
ventilated pizza pan (if using)

Cornmeal for sprinkling pizza peel
(if using)

Extra-virgin olive oil for brushing
crust

5 ounces prosciutto, salami, or other
Italian cold cut, slivered

2 tablespoons Roasted Garlic (page
139), or 2 teaspoons minced
fresh garlic

2 tablespoons minced fresh basil or
flat-leaf parsley

1 1/2 teaspoons minced fresh
oregano, or 1/2 teaspoon
crumbled dried oregano

Salt

Freshly ground black pepper

Calzone

In addition to classic pizza, Naples has given the world the folded stuffed pizza, or calzone. The name means "pant leg" because the original versions were tube shaped, with the dough encasing sausages or salamis, and looked like eighteenth-century men's trouser legs. Almost any pizza topping can be substituted in place of this traditional filling. Some people like to spoon a simple tomato sauce over a calzone when it comes out of the oven.

The recipe makes 4 individual-sized calzone. To make appetizer-sized folded pies, divide the dough into 8 equal pieces and divide the filling equally among the rounds.

Prepare the Seasoned Tomato Pulp or Roasted Tomatoes as directed. If using Roasted Tomatoes, chop coarsely. Set aside to cool to room temperature.

If necessary, review Making Perfect Pizza at Home (pages 9–25).

Make the selected pizza dough and set aside to rise as directed.

In a bowl, combine the mozzarella, ricotta, and 1/4 cup of the Parmesan cheese and set aside.

About 30 minutes before baking the pizza, prepare an oven as directed on page 21 and preheat it to 500 degrees F. If using a pizza screen or ventilated pan, brush it with vegetable oil or coat with spray and set aside. If baking directly on a stone or tiles, sprinkle a pizza peel with cornmeal and set aside.

Divide the dough into 4 equal pieces and form each piece into a ball. Cover loosely with plastic wrap to keep the dough from drying out.

Working with 1 ball at a time, on a lightly floured surface, roll out or stretch the dough into an 8-inch round. Place the dough on the prepared screen, pan, or peel. Brush the dough with olive oil, leaving a 1/2-inch border around the edges, then cover half of the dough round with one-fourth of the cheese mixture, leaving the border around the edges. Distribute one-fourth of the tomato pulp or tomatoes, prosciutto or other meat, garlic, basil or parsley, and oregano over the cheese. Sprinkle with salt and pepper to taste. Fold the uncovered side over the filling and press the edges of the dough together to seal. Brush the dough with olive oil. Repeat with the remaining balls of dough to form as many calzone as will fit into the oven at one time without crowding. If using a pizza peel, give it a quick, short jerk to be sure that the bottom of each crust has not stuck to it.

Transfer the calzone to the preheated oven and bake until the crusts are golden, about 10 minutes.

Remove the calzone to a wire rack and let stand for about 2 minutes, then transfer to a cutting tray or board and lightly brush the crusts with oil. Sprinkle with the remaining 1/4 cup Parmesan cheese and serve immediately.

Makes 4 main-course servings

California-Style Pizza Dough (page 18) or Neapolitan-Style Pizza Dough (page 16)

2 medium-sized heads romaine lettuce, tough outer leaves discarded

Caesar Dressing

2 eggs

3 flat anchovy fillets, rinsed, patted dry, and minced

1½ teaspoons minced garlic

1 teaspoon Dijon mustard

½ cup extra-virgin olive oil

1½ tablespoons freshly squeezed lemon juice, or more if needed

¼ teaspoon salt, or to taste

½ teaspoon freshly ground black pepper, or to taste

Vegetable oil or cooking spray for greasing pizza screen or ventilated pizza pan (if using)

Cornmeal for sprinkling pizza peel (if using)

Extra-virgin olive oil for brushing crust

3 cups freshly shredded high-quality semisoft mozzarella cheese (about 9 ounces), preferably made with whole milk

¼ cup freshly grated Parmesan cheese (about 1 ounce), preferably Parmigiano-Reggiano

Caesar Salad Pizza, Piadina Style

A specialty of Emilia-Romagna along Italy's Adriatic coast, the crust for a *piadina* is traditionally made with baking powder instead of yeast and baked on a hot griddle. After the hot crust comes off the griddle, it is topped with dressed salad greens and/or slices of cold cuts, cheese, and tomato, or spread with chocolate (see page 134). The crust is folded together around the toppings and eaten like a sandwich.

My California version uses regular pizza dough and is inspired by Napa Valley chef Michael Chiarello, who tops his *piadina*-style pizzas with a wide variety of salads combined with grilled meats at his Tomatina restaurants. Use the idea to create your own scrumptious renditions.

Eggs occasionally contain dangerous bacteria that are only killed once the egg and yolk are firmly set. If you prefer not to use the traditional coddled eggs in the Caesar salad dressing, a touch of cream or mayonnaise will add the richness normally provided by the yolks.

If necessary, review Making Perfect Pizza at Home (pages 9–25).

Make the selected pizza dough and set aside to rise as directed.

Tear the lettuce into bite-sized pieces and wash them under cold running water. Place in a salad spinner and spin to remove as much water as possible. Pat dry with paper toweling. Wrap in a cloth kitchen towel or paper toweling and refrigerate for at least 30 minutes to crisp, or place the wrapped leaves in a plastic bag and refrigerate for up to several hours.

To make the Caesar Dressing, bring a small pot of water to a rapid boil over high heat. Place the eggs, one at a time, on a spoon, lower them into the boiling water, and cook for 1 minute. Transfer the eggs to a bowl of cold water to cool. Break the eggs, separating the yolks into a small bowl; discard the whites. Add the anchovies, garlic, mustard, oil, and 1½ tablespoons lemon juice to the yolks and whisk to blend. Whisk in the salt and pepper. Taste and add more lemon juice if needed. Set aside.

About 30 minutes before baking the pizza, prepare an oven as directed on page 21 and preheat it to 500 degrees F. If using a pizza screen or ventilated pan, brush it with vegetable oil or coat with spray and set aside. If baking directly on a stone or tiles, sprinkle a pizza peel with cornmeal and set aside.

Divide the dough into 4 equal pieces and form each piece into a ball. Cover loosely with plastic wrap to keep the dough from drying out.

Working with 1 ball at a time, on a lightly floured surface, roll out or stretch the dough into an 8-inch round. Place the dough on the prepared screen, pan, or peel. Prick the dough all over with a fork and brush it all over with olive oil, then top with one-fourth of the mozzarella, leaving a ½-inch border around the edges. Repeat with the

For another type of pizza "sandwich," bake an unadorned thick crust, then split it horizontally and fill with sliced Italian meats and cheeses.

remaining balls of dough to form as many pizzas as will fit into the oven at one time without crowding. If using a pizza peel, give it a quick, short jerk to be sure that the bottom of each crust has not stuck to it.

Transfer the pizzas to the preheated oven and bake until the crusts are golden, about 10 minutes.

Shortly before the pizzas are done, in a large bowl, combine the chilled lettuce and 2 tablespoons of the Parmesan cheese. Add the dressing to taste and toss well. Set aside.

Remove the pizzas to a wire rack and let stand for about 2 minutes, then transfer to a cutting tray or board and lightly brush the edges of the crusts with olive oil. Mound the salad on the pizzas, dividing evenly, then sprinkle each with the remaining 2 tablespoons Parmesan cheese, dividing evenly, and serve immediately. At the table, instruct diners to fold each pizza in half around

the salad and eat it like a sandwich. For easier eating or sharing, cut each pizza in half with a serrated knife after folding.

Makes 4 main-course servings

California-Style Pizza Dough (page 18) or Neapolitan-Style Pizza Dough (page 16)

2 tablespoons ground dried ancho, pasilla, or other mild to hot chile

2 tablespoons ground cumin

1 tablespoon ground coriander

1 teaspoon crumbled dried oregano

Salt

Freshly ground black pepper

Ground cayenne

1 pound beef skirt or flank steak, trimmed of excess fat and connective tissue

Vegetable oil or cooking spray for greasing grill rack and pizza screen or ventilated pizza pan (if using)

2 large red sweet peppers, stems, seeds, and membranes discarded, cut into wide sections

1 large onion, cut into thick slices

Extra-virgin olive oil for brushing vegetables and crust

1/4 cup freshly squeezed lime juice

Cornmeal for sprinkling pizza peel (if using)

1 1/2 cups freshly shredded yellow Cheddar cheese (about 4 1/2 ounces)

1 1/2 cups freshly shredded Monterey Jack cheese (about 4 1/2 ounces), preferably with chiles added

1/4 cup fresh cilantro (coriander) leaves

Salsa (a favorite recipe or high-quality commercial product) for serving

Fajita Pizza, Piadina Style

In the final decades of the twentieth century, fajitas spread out of Texas to become wildly popular everywhere. In this preparation, a cheesy pizza crust takes the place of the tortilla for wrapping up the flavorful steak. As the steak requires heating up a grill, you may wish to grill the crusts as well (see page 24). Read about *piadine* on page 116.

If necessary, review Making Perfect Pizza at Home (pages 9–25).

Make the selected pizza dough and set aside to rise as directed.

Prepare an open grill for hot direct-heat cooking.

In a small bowl, combine the ground chile, cumin, coriander, oregano, and salt, pepper, and cayenne to taste, and blend well.

Quickly rinse the steak under cold running water and pat dry with paper toweling. Rub the steak all over with the chile mixture and set aside.

When the fire is ready, lightly brush the grill rack with vegetable oil or coat with spray. Brush the sweet peppers and onion with olive oil and place on the rack. Sprinkle the steak with the lime juice and place on the rack. Grill the vegetables, turning occasionally, until tender, 5 to 10 minutes. Grill the steak, turning once, until a meat thermometer inserted from one end into the center of the meat registers 145 degrees F for medium-rare, about 3 minutes per side; do not overcook.

Transfer the steak to a cutting surface, cover loosely with aluminum foil, and let stand for 5 to 10 minutes to reabsorb the juices. Using a sharp

knife held at a diagonal, cut the meat on a bias across the grain into slices about 1/4 inch thick and 3 inches long. Transfer the meat to a bowl. Cut the grilled peppers into narrow strips and cut the onion slices to form half rings, add to the sliced steak, toss together, cover to keep warm, and set aside.

About 30 minutes before baking the pizza, prepare an oven as directed on page 21 and preheat it to 500 degrees F. If using a pizza screen or ventilated pan, brush it with vegetable oil or coat with spray and set aside. If baking directly on a stone or tiles, sprinkle a pizza peel with cornmeal and set aside.

In a bowl, combine the Cheddar and Monterey Jack cheeses and set aside.

Divide the dough into 4 equal pieces and form each piece into a ball. Cover loosely with plastic wrap to keep the dough from drying out.

Working with 1 ball at a time, on a lightly floured surface, roll out or stretch the dough into an 8-inch round. Place the dough on the prepared screen, pan, or peel. Brush the dough all over with olive oil, then top with one-fourth of the cheese mixture, leaving a 1/2-inch border around the edges. Repeat with the remaining balls of dough to form as many pizzas as will fit into the oven at one time without crowding. If using a pizza peel, give it a quick, short jerk to be sure that the bottom of each crust has not stuck to it.

Transfer the pizzas to the preheated oven and bake until the crusts are golden, about 10 minutes.

Remove the pizzas to a wire rack and let stand for about 2 minutes, then transfer to a cutting tray or board and lightly brush the edges of the crusts with olive oil. Mound the steak and vegetable strips on top, sprinkle with the cilantro, and serve immediately. At the table, offer salsa for spooning over the pizzas and instruct diners to fold each pizza in half around the filling and eat it like a sandwich. For easier eating or sharing, cut each pizza in half with a serrated knife after folding.

Makes 4 main-course servings

Pizza pairs well with bubbly beverages: beer, champagne, soda, and sparkling water.

1 tablespoon brown sugar

1 tablespoon paprika

1½ teaspoons freshly ground black
pepper

1½ teaspoons coarse salt

¾ teaspoon ground cayenne

2 pounds boneless pork shoulder
roast (Boston butt)

Liquid smoke

California-Style Pizza Dough
(page 18) or Neapolitan-Style
Pizza Dough (page 16)

Carolina-Style Barbecue Sauce

½ cup apple cider vinegar

3 tablespoons ketchup

1 teaspoon brown sugar, or to taste

¼ teaspoon salt, or to taste

⅛ teaspoon crushed dried chile, or
to taste

Carolina Coleslaw

½ cup mayonnaise

¼ cup distilled white vinegar

2 tablespoons granulated sugar, or
to taste

Salt

Freshly ground black pepper

4 cups finely shredded green cabbage

Vegetable oil or cooking spray for
greasing pizza screen or
ventilated pizza pan (if using)

Cornmeal for sprinkling pizza peel
(if using)

Extra-virgin olive oil for brushing crust

3 cups freshly shredded white Cheddar
cheese (about 9 ounces)

Pulled Pork Pizza, Piadina Style

Inspired by the succulent pork sandwiches of the Carolinas, this unusual pizza is topped with coleslaw tossed with the traditional thin barbecue sauce of the area. Although it can be served as flat pizza with the coleslaw mounded on top, the combination renders a perfect folded *piadina*-style pizza (see page 116).

If you prefer a more traditional approach to my easy oven version of pulled pork, the meat can be slowly cooked in a covered grill or smoker, fueled with hardwood charcoal and soaked fragrant wood chips. Keep the temperature of the cooker around 225 degrees F, adding more charcoal and wood chips as needed, until the pork is done, about 6 hours.

The pork can be prepared and refrigerated a day ahead of making the pizza. The coleslaw can be made ahead and refrigerated for up to 8 hours.

To make the dry rub, in a small bowl, combine all of the rub ingredients and mix well.

Quickly rinse the pork under cold running water and pat dry with paper toweling. Place on a work surface and rub all over with the dry rub. Cover and refrigerate for at least 2 hours or for up to 24 hours; return to room temperature shortly before cooking.

Prepare an oven as directed on page 21, position a rack in the middle of the oven for cooking the pork, and preheat the oven to 525 degrees F.

Place the pork on a sheet of heavy-duty aluminum foil that is large enough to later enclose the pork. Sprinkle liquid smoke lightly over the pork. Bring up the sides of the foil to enclose the meat and seal tightly. Place the package in a baking pan, cover tightly with aluminum foil, transfer to the preheated oven, and bake for 30 minutes.

Reduce the oven temperature to 325 degrees F and continue baking until the meat is very tender and falling apart, about 3½ hours longer.

Meanwhile, if necessary, review Making Perfect Pizza at Home (pages 9–25).

Make the selected pizza dough and set aside to rise as directed.

When the pork is done, remove the pan to a work surface and uncover. Open the foil packet and set the pan aside for the pork to cool in its juices. When the meat is cool enough to handle, shred it into bite-sized pieces and transfer to a bowl.

To make the Carolina-Style Barbecue Sauce, in a small bowl, combine all of the sauce ingredients and mix well. Pour the sauce over the meat and mix well. Cover and refrigerate until needed; return to room temperature and drain off any excess sauce before adding to the pizza.

▶

To make the Carolina Coleslaw, in a bowl, combine the mayonnaise, vinegar, sugar, and salt and pepper to taste. Add the cabbage and toss to blend well. Cover and refrigerate until serving time.

About 30 minutes before baking the pizza, preheat the oven to 500 degrees F. If using a pizza screen or ventilated pan, brush it with vegetable oil or coat with spray and set aside. If baking directly on a stone or tiles, sprinkle a pizza peel with cornmeal and set aside.

Divide the dough into 4 equal pieces and form each piece into a ball. Cover loosely with plastic wrap to keep the dough from drying out.

Working with 1 ball at a time, on a lightly floured surface, roll out or stretch the dough into an 8-inch round. Place the dough on the prepared screen, pan, or peel. Brush the dough all over with olive oil, then top with one-fourth of the cheese, leaving a 1/2-inch border around the

edges. Drain the pulled pork and distribute one-fourth of it over the cheese. Repeat with the remaining balls of dough to form as many pizzas as will fit into the oven at one time without crowding. If using a pizza peel, give it a quick, short jerk to be sure that the bottom of each crust has not stuck to it.

Transfer the pizzas to the preheated oven and bake until the crusts are golden, about 10 minutes.

Remove the pizzas to a wire rack and let stand for about 2 minutes, then transfer to a cutting tray or board and lightly brush the edges of the crusts with olive oil. Drain the coleslaw, spoon it on top of the pizzas, and serve immediately. At the table, instruct diners to fold each pizza in half around the filling and eat it like a sandwich. For easier eating or sharing, cut each pizza in half with a serrated knife after folding.

Makes 4 main-course servings

California-Style Pizza Dough (page 18) or Neapolitan-Style Pizza Dough (page 16)

3/4 cup Roasted Tomatoes (page 137) or peeled, seeded, well-drained, and chopped ripe tomato (see page 12)

2 cups freshly shredded high-quality semisoft mozzarella cheese (about 6 ounces), preferably made with whole milk

1 cup freshly grated Parmesan cheese (about 4 ounces), preferably Parmigiano-Reggiano

1/4 cup minced fresh basil

1 tablespoon minced fresh oregano, or 1 teaspoon crumbled dried oregano

Salt

Olive oil for frying

Deep-Fried Pizza Pockets (Panzarotti)

In previous books, I shared the story of my chance discovery of these fried pies, or *panzarotti*, while strolling the streets of Milan. Throughout Italy, variations on the theme are made daily, wrapped in waxed paper, and eaten out of hand as a snack. Optional additions to the filling of seasoned tomatoes and melted cheese include chopped prosciutto, olives, anchovies, or sun-dried tomatoes.

If necessary, review Making Perfect Pizza at Home (pages 9–25).

Make the selected pizza dough and set aside to rise as directed.

If using Roasted Tomatoes, prepare as directed, chop coarsely, and set aside to cool to room temperature. If using fresh tomato, reserve for later use.

In a bowl, combine the mozzarella and Parmesan cheeses and set aside.

Divide the dough into 8 equal pieces and form each piece into a ball. Cover loosely with plastic wrap to keep the dough from drying out.

Working with 1 ball at a time, on a lightly floured surface, roll out or stretch the dough into a 4-inch round. Distribute 3 tablespoons of the cheese mixture over half of the dough round, leaving a 1/2-inch border around the edges. Sprinkle the tomato, basil, oregano, and salt to taste evenly over the cheese. Top with 3 tablespoons of the remaining cheese mixture. Using a pastry brush, moisten the exposed edges of the dough with water, fold the uncovered half over the filling, and press the edges of the dough together to seal well. Using a wooden skewer or fork, punch several holes along the side opposite the sealed side to allow steam to escape during cooking. Repeat with the remaining balls of dough.

In a deep fryer or dutch oven, pour in oil to a depth of 2 inches and heat to 360 degrees F. Place a wire rack on a baking sheet and position alongside the fryer or stove top. Carefully slip a few *panzarotti* into the hot oil; avoid crowding the pan. Fry, turning frequently, until golden, about 5 minutes. Using tongs or a slotted utensil, transfer the *panzarotti* to the rack to drain well. Fry the remaining *panzarotti* in the same manner, allowing the oil to return to 360 degrees F between batches.

Serve piping hot.

Makes 8 servings

Pizza Pinwheels

Vary this idea by substituting your favorite pizza toppings to create unusual appetizers or snacks.

California-Style Pizza Dough (page 18) or Neapolitan-Style Pizza Dough (page 16)

½ cup Seasoned Tomato Pulp (page 136) or Pizzeria-Style Tomato Sauce (page 138)

2 tablespoons Tapénade (page 71)

Vegetable oil or cooking spray for greasing pizza screen or ventilated pizza pan (if using)

Cornmeal for sprinkling pizza peel (if using)

Extra-virgin olive oil for brushing crust

2 cups freshly shredded high-quality semisoft mozzarella cheese (about 6 ounces), preferably made with whole milk

½ cup freshly grated Parmesan cheese (about 2 ounces), preferably Parmigiano-Reggiano

3 tablespoons minced fresh flat-leaf parsley

If necessary, review Making Perfect Pizza at Home (pages 9–25).

Make the selected pizza dough and set aside to rise as directed.

Prepare the Seasoned Tomato Pulp or Pizzeria-Style Tomato Sauce as directed and set aside to cool to room temperature.

Prepare the Tapénade as directed and set aside.

About 30 minutes before baking the pizza, prepare an oven as directed on page 21 and preheat it to 475 degrees F. If using a pizza screen or ventilated pan, brush it with vegetable oil or coat with spray and set aside. If baking directly on a stone or tiles, sprinkle a pizza peel with cornmeal and set aside.

On a lightly floured surface, roll out or stretch the dough and shape it into a 14-by-12-inch rectangle. Brush the dough all over with olive oil, then spread with a thin layer of the tomato pulp or sauce, leaving a ½-inch border around the edges. Distribute the Tapénade over the tomato layer and sprinkle with the mozzarella cheese. Beginning on one of the shorter sides, tightly fold and press about 1 inch of the dough over the filling. Continue rolling the dough as compactly as possible. Place the rolled dough seam side down on the prepared screen, pan, or peel. If using a pizza peel, give it a quick, short jerk to be sure that the bottom of the crust has not stuck to it.

Transfer the rolled pizza to the preheated oven and bake until the crust is golden, about 12 minutes.

Remove the pizza to a wire rack and let stand for about 5 minutes, then transfer to a cutting tray or board and lightly brush the crust with olive oil. Using a sharp serrated knife, slice crosswise into pieces about ½ inch thick. Sprinkle with the Parmesan cheese and parsley and serve immediately.

Makes 8 servings

Sweet Pizzas

Who says pizza cannot be sweet? When the dough is lightly sweetened and topped with fruit, creamy cheese, and even chocolate, pizza becomes a seductive sweet or, in Italian, *un dolce*, to end a meal. The same combinations also make interesting additions to the American brunch menu, as well as unusual and satisfying snacks. My favorite of these sweet takes on the savory pie is one made with fresh figs and blue cheese drizzled with a bit of honey. It marries perfectly with a glass of wine before dinner or a glass of port or other dessert wine at the end of a meal.

Sweet Pizza Dough (page 20)

1 cup chopped pecans

1 can (14 ounces) sweetened
    condensed milk

Vegetable oil or cooking spray for
    greasing pizza screen or
    ventilated pizza pan (if using)

Cornmeal for sprinkling pizza peel
    (if using)

Melted unsalted butter for brushing
    crust

8 cored fresh or canned pineapple
    slices, well drained

Dulce de Leche Pizzette

At last, the rest of us have caught on to a good thing that has long been a favorite throughout the Spanish-speaking world: *dulce de leche,* or caramelized sweetened milk. It now appears on trendy menus and is featured in a wildly popular ice cream flavor. Here, I've used the smooth sauce to drizzle over hot pineapple and topped it with toasted pecans. Warning: this could become addictive!

The *dulce de leche* can be made ahead, covered, and refrigerated for up to 2 days.

If necessary, review Making Perfect Pizza at Home (pages 9–25).

Make the Sweet Pizza Dough and set aside to rise as directed.

Prepare an oven as directed on page 21, position a rack in the middle of the oven for toasting the pecans and cooking the *dulce de leche,* and pre-heat the oven to 350 degrees F.

To toast the pecans, spread the nuts in a single layer in an ovenproof skillet or baking pan. Toast in the oven, stirring occasionally, until lightly browned and fragrant, 10 to 15 minutes. Transfer the toasted nuts to a plate and set aside to cool completely.

To make the *dulce de leche,* preheat the oven to 425 degrees F. Pour the condensed milk into an 8-inch ovenproof glass casserole or other baking dish and cover tightly with aluminum foil. Place the dish in a larger baking pan and transfer the pan to the oven. Pour enough hot (not boiling) water into the baking pan to come up to the level of the condensed milk in the dish. Bake until the milk is thick and a rich tan, about 1 hour. Check

several times during baking and add hot water as necessary to maintain the water level.

Carefully remove the dish from the baking pan and set aside.

About 30 minutes before baking the pizza, pre-heat the oven to 500 degrees F. If using a pizza screen or ventilated pan, brush it with vegetable oil or coat with spray and set aside. If baking directly on a stone or tiles, sprinkle a pizza peel with cornmeal and set aside.

Divide the dough into 8 equal pieces and form each piece into a ball. Cover loosely with plastic wrap to keep the dough from drying out.

Working with 1 ball at a time, on a lightly floured surface, roll out or stretch the dough into a 4-inch round. Place the dough on the prepared screen, pan, or peel. Prick the dough all over with a fork, brush with melted butter, and top with a pineap-ple slice. Repeat with the remaining balls of dough to form as many *pizzette* as will fit into the oven at one time without crowding. If using a pizza peel, give it a quick, short jerk to be sure that the bottom of each crust has not stuck to it.

▶

Transfer the *pizzette* to the preheated oven and bake until the crusts are golden, about 10 minutes.

Remove the *pizzette* to a wire rack. Spread each *pizzetta* with about 2 tablespoons of the *dulce de leche,* and sprinkle with 2 tablespoons of the toasted pecans. Serve immediately.

Makes 8 servings

New pizzas are global in scope, encompassing toppings from many cuisines that merge happily with Italian traditions.

Sweet Pizza Dough (page 20),
  California-Style Pizza Dough
  (page 18), or Neapolitan-Style
  Pizza Dough (page 16)
1 cup coarsely chopped walnuts
Vegetable oil or cooking spray for
  greasing pizza screen or
  ventilated pizza pan (if using)
Cornmeal for sprinkling pizza peel
  (if using)
Extra-virgin olive oil or walnut oil for
  brushing crust
3 cups crumbled creamy Gorgonzola,
  Cambozola, or other blue
  cheese (about 15 ounces)
About 20 ripe figs, halved lengthwise
High-quality honey for drizzling
Fresh fig leaves for serving (optional)

Fresh Fig, Blue Cheese, and Honey Pizza

Each summer I eagerly await the first harvest of figs so that I can indulge in this exquisite combination of flavors. The idea for this pizza was sparked while enjoying walnut bread spread with blue cheese and topped with figs and honey at the Napa Valley treehouse of my good friend and noted food authority Antonia Allegra. I've topped the pizza with walnuts, but you could add chopped toasted nuts to the dough instead to come closer to Toni's memorable bread. Serve the pizza as a dessert, appetizer, or snack.

If necessary, review Making Perfect Pizza at Home (pages 9–25).

Make the selected pizza dough and set aside to rise as directed.

Prepare an oven as directed on page 21. Place a rack in the center of the oven for toasting the walnuts and preheat the oven to 350 degrees F.

Spread the walnuts in a single layer in an oven-proof skillet or baking pan. Toast in the oven, stirring occasionally, until lightly browned and fragrant, 10 to 15 minutes. Transfer the toasted nuts to a plate and set aside to cool completely.

About 30 minutes before baking the pizza, pre-heat the oven to 500 degrees F. If using a pizza screen or ventilated pan, brush it with vegetable oil or coat with spray and set aside. If baking directly on a stone or tiles, sprinkle a pizza peel with cornmeal and set aside.

On a lightly floured surface, roll out or stretch the dough and shape it as desired. Place the dough on the prepared screen, pan, or peel. Brush the dough all over with olive or walnut oil, then top with the cheese, leaving a ½-inch border around

the edges. Arrange the figs, cut sides up, over the cheese and drizzle with honey to taste. If using a pizza peel, give it a quick, short jerk to be sure that the bottom of the crust has not stuck to it.

Transfer the pizza to the preheated oven and bake until the crust is golden, about 10 minutes.

Remove the pizza to a wire rack and let stand for about 2 minutes, then transfer to a cutting tray or board and lightly brush the edges of the crust with olive or walnut oil. Sprinkle with the toasted walnuts. Slice, place on fig leaves (if using), and serve immediately.

Makes 8 servings

Sweet Pizza Dough (page 20)

¼ cup (½ stick) unsalted butter

½ cup firmly packed light brown
sugar

1 teaspoon ground cinnamon, or to
taste

8 cups thinly sliced, peeled, and
cored apples (see recipe introduction)

Vegetable oil or cooking spray for
greasing pizza screen or
ventilated pizza pan (if using)

Cornmeal for sprinkling pizza peel
(if using)

Melted unsalted butter for brushing
crust

3 cups freshly shredded high-quality
Cheddar cheese (see recipe
introduction)

Apple and Cheddar Pizza

Apples and Cheddar are a classic American pie combination. For this not-too-sweet pizza that makes an unexpected dessert or a good brunch dish, select an excellent Cheddar such as those made in Vermont, Canada, or England. I enjoy the tartness of Granny Smith apples with the cheese, but any flavorful apples that hold their shape after cooking may be used. Consider Baldwin, Cortland, or readily available Golden Delicious.

If necessary, review Making Perfect Pizza at Home (pages 9–25).

Make the Sweet Pizza Dough and set aside to rise as directed.

In a sauté pan or skillet, melt the ¼ cup butter over medium heat. Stir in the brown sugar and cinnamon. Add the apples and cook them, stirring and turning several times, until they are tender but still hold their shape, about 10 minutes. Remove from the heat and set aside to cool to room temperature.

About 30 minutes before baking the pizza, pre-pare an oven as directed on page 21 and preheat it to 500 degrees F. If using a pizza screen or ven-tilated pan, brush it with vegetable oil or cooking spray and set aside. If baking directly on a stone or tiles, sprinkle a pizza peel with cornmeal and set aside.

On a lightly floured surface, roll out or stretch the dough and shape it as desired. Place the dough on the prepared screen, pan, or peel. Prick the dough all over with a fork and brush it with melted butter. Top with the cheese, leaving a ½-inch border around the edges. Drain off any excess liquid from the apples and arrange the

slices in an overlapping pinwheel pattern over the cheese.

Transfer the pizza to the preheated oven and bake until the crust is golden, about 10 minutes.

Remove the pizza to a wire rack and let stand for about 2 minutes, then transfer to a cutting tray or board and lightly brush the edges of the crust with melted butter. Slice and serve immediately.

Makes 8 servings

Sweet Pizza Dough (page 20)

Vegetable oil or cooking spray for greasing pizza screen or ventilated pizza pan

About 3 cups ripe raspberries or hulled strawberries

Sugar

Melted unsalted butter for brushing crust

1 pound cream cheese, cut into small pieces

About 1 cup chocolate sauce (a favorite recipe or high-quality commercial product)

Fresh mint sprigs for garnish

Chocolate and Berry Pizza

A slightly sweet crust oozing with cream cheese and topped with chocolate sauce and seasonal berries is a decadent ending to a meal or makes an unusual afternoon treat. If the strawberries are large, cut them into halves, quarters, or slices.

If necessary, review Making Perfect Pizza at Home (pages 9–25).

Make the Sweet Pizza Dough and set aside to rise as directed.

About 30 minutes before baking the pizza, prepare an oven as directed on page 21 and preheat it to 500 degrees F. Brush a pizza screen or ventilated pizza pan with vegetable oil or coat with spray and set aside. As this pizza must be removed from the oven before the crust is completely set, do not bake directly on a stone or tiles.

In a bowl, lightly sprinkle the berries with sugar to taste and set aside, stirring occasionally, until needed.

On a lightly floured surface, roll out or stretch the dough and shape it as desired. Place the dough on the prepared screen or pan. Prick the dough all over with a fork and brush it with melted butter.

Transfer the pizza to the preheated oven and bake until the crust just begins to brown, about 5 minutes.

Remove the pizza to a work surface and top with the cheese, leaving a ½-inch border around the edges. Return the pie to the oven and continue baking until the crust is golden, about 5 minutes longer.

Meanwhile, gently heat the chocolate sauce and drain the berries.

Remove the pizza to a wire rack and drizzle the warm chocolate sauce over the cheese. Arrange the berries over the cheese, then transfer to a cutting tray or board and lightly brush the edges of the crust with melted butter. Garnish with mint sprigs. Slice and serve immediately.

Makes 8 servings

Neapolitan-Style Pizza Dough
(page 16)
Vegetable oil or cooking spray for
greasing pizza screen or
ventilated pizza pan (if using)
Cornmeal for sprinkling pizza peel
(if using)
Extra-virgin olive oil for brushing
crust
2 cups Nutella spread (see recipe
introduction)

Chocolate-Hazelnut Pizza, Piadina Style

Nutella, a creamy chocolate-hazelnut mixture, is extremely popular in Italy, where a favorite use for the spread is on *piadine* (see page 116). I think this pizza could become wildly popular here.

If necessary, review Making Perfect Pizza at Home (pages 9–25).

Make the Neapolitan-Style Pizza Dough and set aside to rise as directed.

About 30 minutes before baking the pizza, prepare an oven as directed on page 21 and preheat it to 500 degrees F. If using a pizza screen or ventilated pan, brush it with vegetable oil or coat with spray and set aside. If baking directly on a stone or tiles, sprinkle a pizza peel with cornmeal and set aside.

Divide the dough into 4 equal pieces and form each piece into a ball. Cover loosely with plastic wrap to keep the dough from drying out.

Working with 1 ball at a time, on a lightly floured surface, roll out or stretch the dough into an 8-inch round. Place the dough on the prepared screen, pan, or peel. Prick the dough all over with a fork and brush it all over with olive oil. Repeat with the remaining balls of dough to form as many pizzas as will fit into the oven at one time without crowding. If using a pizza peel, give it a quick, short jerk to be sure that the bottom of each crust has not stuck to it.

Transfer the pizzas to the preheated oven and bake until the crusts are golden, about 10 minutes.

Remove the pizzas to a wire rack and let stand for about 2 minutes, then transfer to a cutting tray or board and lightly brush the edges of the crusts with olive oil. Spread ¼ cup of the Nutella on each pizza and serve immediately. Instruct diners to fold each pizza in half around the filling and eat it like a sandwich. For easier eating or sharing, cut each pizza in half with a serrated knife after folding.

Makes 4 servings

Basics

Seasoned Tomato Pulp

This preparation approximates the flavor of fresh tomatoes that are exposed to the intense heat of a wood-burning pizza oven. When delicious vine-ripened tomatoes are plentiful, you may wish to prepare the pulp in quantity and freeze in small batches for up to several months. My recipe calls for meaty plum tomatoes, but other flavorful varieties may be used. Because they carry additional juice, you may need 2 pounds or more to equal the same yield. At other times, canned tomatoes are preferable to bland supermarket versions.

You'll have enough pulp to moderately cover a full recipe of pizza dough. If you enjoy more tomatoes on your pies, you may wish to double the recipe, especially since leftover pulp is good for many uses.

> 1¼ pounds ripe plum tomatoes, or 1 can
> (28 ounces) high-quality peeled
> tomatoes packed in tomato juice or
> puree
> 3 tablespoons extra-virgin olive oil
> 1 teaspoon minced garlic (optional)
> Salt

If using fresh tomatoes, bring a pot of water to a boil over high heat and ready a large bowl of iced water. Using a sharp knife, cut out and discard the stems and surrounding hard cores from the tomatoes. Carefully drop the tomatoes, a few at a time, into the boiling water and blanch for about 30 seconds. Using a slotted utensil, remove the tomatoes to the bowl of iced water and let stand for about 2 minutes. Transfer the tomatoes to a work surface. Using your fingertips, pull off the skins from the cored ends to peel the tomatoes. Slice each tomato in half horizontally and squeeze each half with your hand over a sink or bowl to release the seeds and juices; you may need to use your fingers to scrape some of the seeds out of the cavities. Discard the seeds and juices.

If using canned tomatoes, pour through a strainer set over a sink or bowl to remove the juices. If the tomatoes are whole, slice each one in half horizontally and squeeze each half with your hand over the sink or bowl to release the seeds and juices; you may need to use your fingers to scrape some of the seeds out of the cavities. If the tomatoes are already cut, use your fingers to remove as many of the seeds as possible. Discard the seeds and juices.

Using a sharp knife, chop the drained tomatoes, or transfer them to a food processor and blend to a chunky puree.

In a saucepan, heat the oil over medium heat. Add the garlic (if using) and cook, stirring frequently, until soft but not browned, about 1 minute. Add the tomatoes and cook, uncovered, stirring occasionally, until almost all of the liquid is evaporated, 15 to 20 minutes. Season to taste with salt and set aside to cool to room temperature.

Use immediately, or cover and refrigerate for up to 1 week; return to room temperature before using.

Makes about 1 cup

Roasted Tomatoes

Roasting draws out excess moisture from tomatoes that can turn a pizza crust soggy and improves the flavor of less-than-perfect specimens, making them sweet and tangy. The problem is that these are so delicious that you'll be tempted to eat them all before they make it to the pizza. Indeed, it is a good idea to make extra just for snacking.

> 1½ pounds ripe plum tomatoes or other
>   meaty flavorful tomatoes such as
>   Beefsteak
> Extra-virgin olive oil for brushing or
>   drizzling over tomatoes
> Salt

Preheat an oven to 250 degrees F.

Bring a pot of water to a boil over high heat and ready a large bowl of iced water. Using a sharp knife, cut out and discard the stems and surrounding hard cores from the tomatoes. Carefully drop the tomatoes, a few at a time, into the boiling water and blanch for about 30 seconds. Using a slotted utensil, remove the tomatoes to the bowl of iced water and let stand for about 2 minutes. Transfer the tomatoes to a work surface. Using your fingertips, pull off the skins from the cored ends to peel the tomatoes. Slice plum tomatoes in half lengthwise, or slice round tomatoes into quarters. Squeeze each piece with your hand over a sink or a bowl to release the seeds and juices; you may need to use your fingers to scrape some of the seeds out of the cavities. Discard the seeds and juices.

Using a small, sharp knife, remove most of the inside flesh, leaving only the thick exterior portion.

Arrange the tomatoes, cut sides down, in a single layer on rimmed baking sheets and press each piece down lightly to flatten. Brush or drizzle generously with oil. Sprinkle lightly with salt. Transfer to the oven and roast for 1 hour, then turn the tomatoes, baste with a little more oil and any collected juices, sprinkle with salt to taste, and continue roasting until very soft, reduced in size, and slightly wrinkled but still moist, about 1 hour longer. Watch carefully near the end of cooking to avoid burning the edges.

Remove the baking sheets to a work surface and let the tomatoes cool to room temperature.

Cut the tomatoes as directed in individual recipes and use immediately, or cover and refrigerate for up to 4 days; return to room temperature before using.

Makes about 1 cup

Pizzeria-Style Tomato Sauce

This recipe makes about twice as much sauce as needed for most of my recipes, but I want there to be plenty for those who like extra sauce. And leftover sauce keeps in the refrigerator for up to a week or in the freezer for several months.

If you have access to meaty, flavorful tomatoes during their season, you may wish to make this sauce in quantity and freeze it. I use plum tomatoes that have been bred for cooking and are meaty with only a little juice. Other flavorful varieties can be used, but you'll probably need at least 3 pounds to yield the same quantity of sauce.

When good fresh tomatoes are not available, the sauce is best made with high-quality canned tomatoes (see page 12). Purchase whole peeled tomatoes or ready-cut ones.

> 2 pounds ripe plum tomatoes, or 1 can (28 ounces) high-quality peeled tomatoes packed in tomato juice or puree
> 3 tablespoons extra-virgin olive oil
> 1 teaspoon minced garlic
> 3 tablespoons tomato paste
> 1 tablespoon minced fresh oregano, or 1 teaspoon crumbled dried oregano
> Salt
> Crushed dried chile

If using fresh tomatoes, bring a pot of water to a boil over high heat and ready a large bowl of iced water. Using a sharp knife, cut out and discard the stems and surrounding hard cores from the tomatoes. Carefully drop the tomatoes, a few at a time, into the boiling water and blanch for about 30 seconds. Using a slotted utensil, remove the tomatoes to the bowl of iced water and let stand for about 2 minutes. Transfer the tomatoes to a work surface. Using your fingertips, pull off the skins from the cored ends to peel the tomatoes. Slice each tomato in half horizontally and squeeze each half with your hand over a strainer set in a bowl to release the seeds into the strainer and collect the juice into the bowl; you may need to use your fingers to scrape some of the seeds out of the cavities. Discard the seeds and save the juice. Place the tomatoes on a cutting surface, chop coarsely, add them to the juice in the bowl, and set aside.

If using canned tomatoes, strain the juice from the tomatoes into a bowl and set aside. If the tomatoes are whole, slice each one in half horizontally and squeeze each half with your hand over a sink or bowl to release the seeds; you may need to use your fingers to scrape some of the seeds out of the cavities. Place the tomatoes on a cutting surface, chop coarsely, add them to the juice in the bowl, and set aside. If the tomatoes are chopped, use your fingers to remove as many of the seeds as possible. Add the tomatoes to the juice in the bowl and set aside.

In a saucepan, heat the oil over medium heat. Add the garlic and cook, stirring occasionally, until soft but not browned, about 1 minute. Add the tomatoes and juice, tomato paste, oregano, and salt and crushed chile to taste. Bring to a boil, then adjust the heat to maintain a simmer and simmer, uncovered, stirring frequently, until flavorful and thickened, 20 to 30 minutes.

Transfer the sauce to a food processor and puree until fairly smooth. Taste and add more salt, oregano, and chile if needed. Set aside to cool to room temperature.

Use immediately, or cover and refrigerate for up to 1 week; return to room temperature before using.

Makes about 2 cups

Roasted Garlic

Roasting transforms pungent garlic into a sweet and creamy sensation that makes a great addition to pizza.

> Whole garlic heads
> Olive oil
> Salt

Preheat an oven to 350 degrees F.

Cut off and discard the top one-fourth of each garlic head to expose individual cloves. Peel away most of the outer papery skin, leaving the heads intact. Place in a baking dish, generously drizzle or rub the cut surfaces with olive oil, and sprinkle with salt to taste. Cover with aluminum foil and bake for 45 minutes, then uncover and roast until soft, about 15 minutes longer.

Squeeze the tender cloves from their papery sheaths into a bowl. Use as directed in recipes.

Roasted Chiles or Sweet Peppers

Both chiles and sweet peppers are great toppings for pizza. Roasting brings out their optimal flavor.

> Fresh mild to hot chiles or sweet peppers

Place whole chiles or sweet peppers on a grill rack over a charcoal fire, directly over a gas flame, or under a preheated broiler. Roast, turning several times, until the skin is charred on all sides; the timing will depend on the intensity and proximity of the heat. Transfer to a bowl, cover, and let stand for about 10 minutes.

Alternatively, cut off and discard the stem ends and discard the seeds and membranes. Following the natural contours of the chiles or peppers, cut horizontally into wide strips that are as flat as possible. Place the strips, skin sides up, on a baking sheet and roast under a preheated broiler until the skin is charred all over. Transfer to a bowl, cover, and let stand for about 10 minutes.

After roasting by either of the preceding methods, using your fingertips or a small, sharp knife, rub or scrape away the charred skin from the chiles or sweet peppers; do not rinse. If roasted whole, cut off and discard the stem ends and discard the seeds and membranes.

Use as directed in recipes.

East Coast diners generally favor medium-thick pizzas topped with traditional tomato sauce, mozzarella cheese, and vegetables or meats.

Index

Recipe Index

Table of Equivalents

The exact equivalents in the following tables have been rounded for convenience.

Oven Temperature

Fahrenheit	Celsius	Gas
250	120	1/2
275	140	1
300	150	2
325	160	3
350	180	4
375	190	5
400	200	6
425	220	7
450	230	8
475	240	9
500	260	10

Liquid/Dry Measures

U.S.	Metric
1/4 teaspoon	**1.25** milliliters
1/2 teaspoon	**2.5** milliliters
1 teaspoon	**5** milliliters
1 tablespoon (3 teaspoons)	**15** milliliters
1 fluid ounce (2 tablespoons)	**30** milliliters
1/4 cup	**60** milliliters
1/3 cup	**80** milliliters
1/2 cup	**120** milliliters
1 cup	**240** milliliters
1 pint (2 cups)	**480** milliliters
1 quart (4 cups, 32 ounces)	**960** milliliters
1 gallon (4 quarts)	**3.84** liters
1 ounce (by weight)	**28** grams
1 pound	**454** grams
2.2 pounds	**1** kilogram

Length

U.S.	Metric
1/8 inch	**3** millimeters
1/4 inch	**6** millimeters
1/2 inch	**12** millimeters
1 inch	**2.5** centimeters